The Intention Idea

MELISSA CANTRELLE

Copyright © 2020 Melissa Cantrelle

All rights reserved.

ISBN: 978-1-7346965-0-9

Cover image © Delphotostock / stock.adobe.com
Author Photo by Dan Coppersmith

DEDICATION

For Merla

CONTENTS

Preface	vii
Part 1: Conversation	1
Part 2: Tools	60
Part 3: Follow Your Heart	110
Part 4: Application	166
Resources	218

PREFACE

I love to write. I love the flow of pen on paper and the transference of ideas into words that can be shared across time and space. When I was in elementary school, I wrote short stories – things like "The Day I Became A Giant" and "How To Make Elephant Stew." When I was a teenager, my mom introduced me to the art of automatic writing as a way of communicating with parts of myself – a technique known as Voice Dialogue. That exploration progressed into automatic writing to communicate with Light Beings - a group of high vibration beings I intentionally asked questions of and received guidance and perspectives that felt different than my own inner thoughts. All of this automatic writing was very personal – pages upon pages of journaling I used for my own life navigation.

Then in my early thirties, I traveled to Yosemite National Park several times for lengthy camping trips, lots of hiking, and lots of photography of the inspiring nature there. I felt very connected to the rocks, trees, waterfalls, high alpine lakes, and meadows. When I came home from one of those trips and looked at some of the photos, they called to me in a new way. It felt like they had a message to share with humanity and I was a potential vehicle for them to get their message out. So I did automatic writing to channel in the messages from the Nature spirits that were represented by the photos I had taken. That was my first published book: *Conversations With Nature*.

Since then, there have been several life changes: the addition of a life partner to walk the path with me, a cross-country move and back again, businesses started, closed and still running, several other books written, and lots of self-development courses. Along the way, I dove deeper and deeper into the Law of Attraction and how to work with visions and visualization in order to manifest dreams and achieve goals.

My new life partner was already an Avatar® Master & Wizard[1]

---

[1] Avatar®, ReSurfacing® and Enlightened Planetary Civilization® are registered trademarks of Star's Edge, Inc. All rights reserved.

(which means he was skilled at manifesting intentions) and he was interested in helping people increase their self-esteem. As we explored combining self-esteem practices with visioning practices, we felt we were on the right track for raising our vibrations *during* the process of manifesting intentions. We felt more aligned with the flow of life, and the people attending our small-group workshops also seemed more at ease with their own vision manifesting journeys.

And then I took the Avatar Course. This course teaches a series of experiential exercises that enable you to eliminate limiting beliefs and self-doubt, and to deliberately create an authentic life. Everything in the course aligned beautifully with what I was exploring, and I was able to finally make forward movement in areas of my life that had been really stuck.

In 2013 I became a licensed Avatar Master and began helping guide people through the Avatar Course. Six months later, I took the Avatar Wizards Course and was blown away by the fast and easy integration of life-long challenges, and by the grace I felt in this Universal flow of creating and discreating. While I had been a student and teacher of Law of Attraction principles for many years, all of the Avatar materials and courses took my understanding and experience of intention work to a whole new level.

You will see me reference Avatar several times in this book because the tools have become an integral part of my life and my ways of managing my consciousness. My understanding of intentions and how to work with them advanced exponentially thanks to my Avatar experiences, and I'm sure I would not have been as good of a vehicle for the Intention Idea if I had not already taken the Avatar Courses[2]. My gratitude is boundless for Harry Palmer for creating the Avatar materials and for the entire Avatar network for helping our planet integrate these tools.

A Note About Exploring Avatar
The Avatar Course materials after the initial 2-day ReSurfacing® workshop are necessarily confidential and only available to

---

[2] The content in this book is my own and does not represent Star's Edge International's positions, strategies or opinions.

individuals who take the Avatar Course under guidance of an Avatar Master. These are sacred, powerful tools for creation that require personal introduction and attentiveness to your integration. If you have an inkling that you might want to explore these tools, I highly encourage you to find an Avatar Master who resonates with you and ask them to introduce you to the Avatar materials. You can also start by reading some of Harry Palmer's books: *The Avatar Path*, *Living Deliberately*, *Private Lessons*, *The Avatar Legacy*, and the public exercises in the *ReSurfacing* workbook[3].

So here I am now, feeling the call to write again and still enjoying the ongoing exploration of what we humans can do when we master our use of consciousness to create intentions. For the last year or more (I don't have a pinpointed day when this idea came in), I've been feeling like there's something about intentions that I'm supposed to bring into the world. Honestly, I'm still not sure if I can define it. Anyway, that's how this got started – I got curious.

I happened across Elizabeth Gilbert's book *Big Magic* and fell in love with her concept of ideas roaming the earth and hoping for a human to help them manifest. I decided to make a list of the ideas that were currently in my awareness as wanting me to manifest them, and at the top of my list was this thing I called "the Intention Idea." When I used my mind to try to figure it out, I didn't get very far. Thankfully, I felt inspired to treat it as a consciousness separate from me and I started a conversation to try to find out more about what it is and what it's about. That's how this began…

---

[3] You can find all of Harry Palmer's current books here: https://avatarbookstore.com/

PART 1

CONVERSATION

DAY 1

Me: What is the Intention Idea that wants to manifest through me?

Intention Idea (II): Helping people to harness their intentions to create a kinder world.

Me: Why kinder?

II: Because kindness implies harmony / harmonic order.

Me: Why is that important?

II: The more ordered and in harmony the world is, the more ideas can manifest, the more expansion of awareness across all time and space.

Me: Why is intention so important? Why not creation?

II: Because intention is the unseen part of creation that is overlooked. If you only look at creation, you will be blocked sometimes for not having addressed underlying intentions.

Me: How can we best work together?

II: Keep listening to me. Be aware of me. Yes, this dialog is good, but not the only way. Keep your attention on me lightly. Keep open to other perspectives of me. Let it *all* gel in your ways of seeing and communication.

Do not be concerned if you see me coming through someone else at the same time – the world can handle and appreciate the vastness of the Intention Idea through many channels.

Me: What's my next step with you?

II: Don't push the river. Let it Flow, simmer, trickle, gurgle, stagnate, swirl, and gush as it will.

Me: Can I make a sketch of you?

II: If it helps, but it won't stay the same.

Me: Why not?

II: Because what needs to be said / taught / communicated / shared about intentions is changing over time.

Me: How do I start helping you manifest?

II: Right Question! [Beaming] This dialog helps. Now go walk and muse about intentions. Trust me. ☺

* * *

Me: I went for a walk and mused on the question "where does intention come from?" Here are some of the answers and perspectives that came to me:
- I don't know
- Higher Self
- Desire to experience something
- Contrast
- Desire and Resistance
- An Identity
- Feels like it directs the resource of attention

At the end of my walk I concluded:

I don't know how I got it, but it's a blessing I'd like to make the most of and use well.

DAY 2

Me: How do I best keep working with you to help you manifest? Is it OK to keep doing this dialog?

II: As long as you don't get attached to it, it's a good place to start.

Me: What else should I be asking you?

II: Whatever your heart desires.

Me: Is that where intention comes from? My heart's desires?

II: Sometimes. It's usually a good starting place. It will at least help you unwind the pre-existing intentions you have stored up. And, in the long run, your heart's desires will guide you toward your soul's path – in alignment with your Higher Self.

Me: Is it OK to do mostly automatic writing to help you manifest? It feels weird to not use my mind and figure it out. I'm also worried what I'll seem like to others if I have a *second* book of channeled writing.

II: You're getting ahead of yourself. Don't assume that what is now will always be. Be with this writing form now, because it feels good and it works. It also helps you stay in your heart and out of your mind. That's important for working with intention. ☺

Me: Will you manifest as a book? Or …? Do you know what you want to be when you grow up? ☺

II: Exactly. You're questioning my form just like asking a kid what

THE INTENTION IDEA

they want to be when they grow up. It's too soon, too much pressure. And maybe they (I) want to be many things, to have a variety of experiences not limited to one label of being-ness.

Me: My mind has a lot of questions. Like how long it's going to take to manifest you? How much will I have to write before I'm done? (My hand is already sore from writing). Where is this going? What will it look like? Will it really come to fruition?

II: Sounds a lot like the questions a mind always asks when you hold an intention and you haven't manifested it yet.

It's like a grey zone between inception and birth, where you have to hold the most faith in the outcome while the manifesting takes its time to process.

Me: What do I best do with my mind and its questions during this time?

II: Let it be. Let it do its thing. Don't get attached to any of its answers. Do your best to stay present with what-is, in this moment. Enjoy the process of manifesting and see it as that – "the process of manifesting."

Me: Feels a little like the process of writing my first book.

II: Yes! Like when you were writing your book and you decided to label the time you spent walking and thinking about your book as "writing time."

Manifesting is not always as you think it ought to appear. It's not always quick. Or Magical. Sometimes (often) you have to keep showing up and doing "the work" to help things keep moving forward.

Many people get excited about manifesting when the end result /

desired outcome appears, and do not feel so excited when they are in process, in-between, or still working on it.

It would be nice if you could just shift your perspective to be excited about, and enjoy, the part of the process where no outer physical world evidence exists yet, but you *feel* your intention, your alignment with it, and trust that everything is going to work out all right.

If you could and would, please, shift your focus of attention to enjoyment of the process, it would be easier for *everyone* (ideas and intentions included) to grow and birth into the world.

Me: Sounds like being pregnant with an idea or intention.

II: Yes, like pregnancy: don't try to rush the nine months, but enjoy all the aspects, shifts, and changes as your manifesting process evolves.

Don't Push The River.
☺

Me: I feel a little sadness that my mind won't be doing much to bring you to the world – to organize and plan and think about intentions. I feel like I'm not doing much, not responsible for much, when I automatic-write / channel what you have to say.

II: It's true. You as an ego-mind are not responsible for figuring it out.

What your mind is really asking though, is how it can take credit. Where and when will it get approval, praise, and appreciation for how you brought me into the world. Your mind can't take credit for who I am, or what I have to say. That's all me (filtered through you, but ideally with as little of you, and as much of me, as possible).

Me: What do you suggest I do with the sadness?

II: Let it go. 🙏

No really, let it go.

Just like meditating, your job is to watch the thoughts as they pass – be an observer – and let them go where they will. When you are observing, rather than trying to control, you are aligning with and identifying with your observer self that is not the mind or the thinker, but rather is the Higher Self.

That is enough.

You are always good enough.
♡ 🙏

DAY 3

Me: What's the best way to use intention / to work with intention?

II: There is no *best* way, but there are many good, helpful, and supportive ways.

Working with intention is like working with one of your senses – sight, hearing, touch, taste, smell. The more you pay attention to it, the finer tuned your sense will be, and the more ways you can apply it.

Also, intention is like a sense because it works with unseen / hidden qualities.

Well, they are only hidden and un-sensed until you refine your senses to perceive better.

Me: If intention is like a sense, what am I tuning into, and what do I do with it?

II: You are tuning in to your Higher Self and the Cosmic Flow of The Universe.

What you do with it is up to you, and ideally in alignment with the Cosmic Flow and ever-unfolding expansion of the Universe.

To feel for an intention that aligns with your next evolutionary step, you can ask yourself "What brings the most Joy, here and now." Or you can ask, "How can I show up more?" Or, "How can I be of better service to our World?"

The key to tuning in to your intention is to tune in to the Higher Vibration part of yourself that is always aligned and tuned in harmony with the Universe.

THE INTENTION IDEA

Getting out of your little ego mind is usually a good first step.

Me: It feels like intention is something I can point at things – like a laser beam that attracts and manifests things into physical creation. That's why we have the jokes "watch where you point that thing" and "be careful what you wish for" – because we really are powerful creators. So how do we (I) learn how to better point and aim our intentions?

II: Well, first be careful with the laser beam analogy, because I don't want you to get the idea that it is always so direct and pointed to work with intention. Sometimes it is a more diffuse and broad light direction. Like, sometimes your intention will act as a lighthouse beacon. And sometimes it will be like the glow of a city at night. The point is, don't judge the quality of the directness of your intention – just feel what it is for you in any given moment. (Yes, it can change over time.)

So how you aim it isn't quite as relevant now that you see it's not always a direct beam of manifesting energy. Nevertheless, I will tell you how to work with it.

As I've said, you can work with it by feeling its quality in the moment. Tune in and feel what kind of light your intention is now. Feel if it is pointing in a direction, or calling things to you, or just generally beaming and glowing.

You are powering this light with your own energies of desire, appreciation, passion, excitement, and joy. The quality of your energy affects the quality of the light of your intention. And *YOU* can impact and control the quality of your energy with your choice of attitudes, thoughts, and beliefs.

Start there.

DAY 4

Me: How is intention different than a thought or a belief? Or is it the same?

II: Thoughts and beliefs are related to intentions, but not the same. You can feel the difference in what it's like to have passing or idle thoughts, versus what it's like to be thinking with more energy about something you want to create. The energy in, behind, and powering the thought is core to the intention. It's not *all* of what an intention is, but it's most of it.

Thoughts can come and go, but the quality of the energy behind the thought determines if it is an intention.

No energy – like no interest – has no intention. Lots of energy – whether as a strong desire or a strong resistance – has lots of intention.

But it can also be strong, powerful energy that isn't in the quality of desire or resistance. You might call it an unbiased energy. I would call it Universal energy – the energy of the Universe.

This Universal energy creates for the joy of creating, expanding, and experiencing – not out of need/want/desire/attraction or dislike/hate/resistance/repulsion.

It is a fine art to direct and use your intentions from Universal energy. Most humans live in the polarity between desire and resistance, and they rarely experience the perspective of pure Universal energy. Nevertheless, it is fully accessible to everyone – it's what you are made of.

Me: What about beliefs? How is intention different than a belief?

THE INTENTION IDEA

II: Beliefs play well (mostly) with intention because they help you to have faith that something is happening when you don't yet see the results. A belief can also hold you back from manifesting your intention if it's a limiting belief. The intention is the underlying energy of what you want to create – the direction you want to go in – and the flavor of Universal expansion and experience you are focusing on.

If intention was the ocean, beliefs would be any kind of cup, glass, or container you use to scoop up some ocean water. It's still the ocean/intention inside the container/belief, but often you are more cognizant of the outer container and its qualities than what's inside.

So yeah, they play together, intentions and beliefs, but they are not the same thing. One is more like an energy (intention) and the other is more like a conduit (beliefs).

DAY 5

Me: I'm curious how we learn to work with intention? In my qigong class, the instructor talks about acting with intention, acting with confidence that we are doing what we say or think we are doing, and not trying to visualize it. As he says it, "it's fine if visualization happens, but you're not trying to visualize or force how the energy flows." So, I guess my question is, how do we learn this use of intention that is not thinking, believing, or visualizing?

II: It's natural. It's part of your evolution as a human being. Just like it's natural to learn to use your body to move around in the physical world, it's natural to learn to use your will to direct your attention and intend for movement in the unseen / quantum world. (Really, I mean the quantum soup that crosses between the unseen energetic world and the physically manifested world of matter.)

Me: Can we accelerate and improve our learning and use of intention?

II: Yes of course. Anything you put your attention on will grow. So, putting attention on intention will grow your senses and abilities – will fine tune them.

Me: Is that it? Just put more attention on it to get better at it?

II: Pretty much. It's like your qigong teacher would say – just keep practicing the moves to whatever your ability and it will keep getting easier.

Me: Sounds like a recipe for life?

II: Not my department, but definitely helpful for increasing your intention skills.

Me: What about Power? Your ocean analogy makes me think of intention as a vast power source – or maybe something that requires power in order to move it? Like the powerful gravity of the moon moves the tides, or an earthquake creates a tidal wave. How does power relate to intention?

II: There is much to say about this. Power in itself is a deep and broad topic to cover. Let's just talk about how *your* power influences *your* intention for now.

Me: OK. How does my power influence my intention?

II: The more clear Power you have (not force, not power affected by limiting beliefs or strong desires – but clear, Universal energy power you tap into without restrictions), then the more intentions you can create. Bigger intentions, more intentions, more "irons in the fire" as you say, and more "achieving the impossible," which really means doing what you couldn't *see* could be done.

Me: How do I access more clear, Universal energy to better fuel my intentions?

II: You know the answers: clear away limiting beliefs, clean up stuck attention on past (or present, or future) impressions, and align your thoughts, attitudes, and actions with a greater goal that is in harmony with the Universal Direction of expansion and exploration.

Me: So keep going? Keep practicing at whatever ability I can right now?

II: You know it! ☺

DAY 6

Me: What's the effect of combining my intentions with other people's intentions? I just finished reading *The Field* (by Lynne McTaggart) and a lot of the experiments in the quantum field seemed to report that people who were connected in some way – "a bonded couple" or even just people who had a chance to get to know each other – had more impact. They were better able to remote view across time and space and were better able to influence the random number generators in the experiments.

Is this an effect of increased power (Universal energy)? Or what's really happening when two or more people are working together on the same intention?

II: It's a combination of things that causes greater impact when more than one person holds an intention. Yes, there is a greater supply of Universal energy. There is also greater alignment with and interest in this direction of Universe unfoldment and exploration.

It's like when you see a school of fish or a flock of birds change direction. Sometimes there are just one or two birds choosing to go a little bit different direction, and soon more or even all of the flock are going that way too. There is an alignment of energies in co-creating this directional experience.

Me: If I want to steer my experiences in a different direction, how do I get more birds to fly in a new direction with me?

II: Well, you don't have to get the birds (or people) around you to go in the same direction as you and your intentions. You can also easily be a solo bird having a unique experience that is not as *obviously* shared in the present moment with those around you.

And, if your intention is to share your experience with "your flock," then your new direction must be aligned with the greater, bigger-picture intention of the flock.

It doesn't need to make logical sense, but at an energetic, vibrational-feel level, your intention must align with greater flock intentions in order for the flock to flow with you and your intention.

Me: What's the difference between having an individual intention and an intention for a bigger group – like for society, humanity, or our world?

II: When you are focusing your energy on an "individual" intention, you are already, always, having an impact on the Whole of society, humanity, the world, and the Universe.

Every intention you hold has an impact on the greater sea of intention energies and on Universe unfoldment.

When you are focused on a Bigger Picture intention – like what you wish for all of humanity, or for your known society – you are more obviously combining your intention with those in that "flock." You are more clearly aligning and contributing to a group intention, and acting as a bigger organism of coherent intention.

Both types of intention are extremely valuable parts of intention-work, life, and the Universe's unfoldment. One is not better than the other. And it is ideal when you hold both types of intention: "individual" and "communal."

Me: What's the effect of holding an intention for World Peace? How much is my intention doing to actually bring about World Peace? Is there something else I should be doing to make it happen?

II: Your intention for World Peace has more impact than you're likely to realize.

When you hold a World Peace intention you are aligning your

thoughts, attitudes, and vibrational energies with this greater-good goal. From this place, you open yourself, those around you, and those connected through you, to new possibilities and paths of opportunity for further creating World Peace.

The saying "it starts with you" is true because each person on the planet has immediate control over their own energy vibration and creational direction / evolutionary direction. When you point yourself toward World Peace that's one more bird in the flock flying in that direction.

As for what else you can do to make it happen, the most important thing is to keep holding your intention and listening for the Universal whispers of what's next. Sometimes your next step is to be kind to the person directly in front of you. Sometimes your next step is to organize a larger group's actions and thoughts toward World Peace. Do not judge the Universe's whispers as too big, too small, not contributing enough, not that important, or whatever other silly ideas your mind comes up with. Just do whatever is in front of you with your World Peace intention in your heart. And maybe *trust* that *that* is enough to manifest it.

Oh, also, intentions do not manifest in time and space the way physical world cause and effect changes happen. In the physical world, you hammer a nail into two boards and they stick together. Cause: you hammering a nail. Effect: boards stick together now. In the Quantum realms of intention, you hold an intention and the effect is everywhere, omnipresent across time and space. But in physical manifestation, you may or may not see an obvious effect yet. Sometimes sea changes in the Intention ocean have other colliding flows to work out before a physical manifestation of your newest intention is visible.

You are still, always, having an effect on the Universe with your intentions. If you do not yet have physical world manifestation of your intention, then keep holding the intention, clearing away limiting beliefs, removing stuck attention on interfering intentions, and following the Universe's whispers for what physical world actions to take next.

DAY 7

Me: Why is intention something you can set and let it work without having to keep enforcing it? And why do I sometimes need to put my intention back in – re-state it or re-align with it?

II: Imagine a sea of waves. Each intention you create is a wave heading for shore. Once you have given the initial push in a direction with your life-force energy, that intention-wave is in motion and will reach the shore – it will manifest.

Unless … another wave comes along and interrupts it. Or you are so far from shore that when your wave hits, it is barely noticeable – maybe even swallowed up in other, more obvious intention waves.

So that's when you might give another push to your intention-wave. The interesting thing about this analogy is you can also see how applying more life-force energy – more of your Universal Power – will make an intention wave go faster and farther. And when you don't have enough life-force energy to create the desired effect, you can give another push. You can also do more to free up your attention and have better access to more Universal energy.

Yes, I'm quite pleased with this analogy – I hope it will help you to relax any judgments and frustrations you have when an intention needs to be re-stated or takes longer to manifest than you prefer. It's a sea of intentions you are playing with – lighten up! ☺

* * *

Me: I got curious about the distinction between intention and attention, so I looked up their definitions and etymology. Here's what I found:

THE INTENTION IDEA

Intention comes from the word intend.
In (toward) + tendere (stretch or tend, like tend in a direction)
Originates in Latin from intendere (intend, extend, direct)
Then became Old French: entendre (hear, understand, learn, know)
Then became Old English: entend (direct the attention to)
Today's definition of intend: have (a course of action) as one's purpose or objective.

Attention comes from the word attend.
Ad (to) + tendere (stretch)
Originates in Latin from attendere (to stretch in a direction)
Then became Old French: attendre (expect, wait, hope, watch)
Then became Middle English: attend (apply one's mind / one's energies to)
And today's definition of attend: be present at, deal with, occur as a result of.
Today's definition of attention: notice taken of something, regarding it as important / interesting, taking special care of something.

DAY 8

Me: Why am I talking to Intention Idea and not straight to Intention? What's the difference?

II: Using the name "Intention Idea" helps you separate and distinguish the specific Intention Idea meant to come through you. If you opened yourself to talk to "Intention" you might hear from other people's intentions, your intentions, or just a general confusion of "who do you want to talk to?" It would be like saying "Hey, human!" to a crowd. You might get a variety of responses or none.

Me: So why are you called "Intention Idea"?

II: I'm not really. But it's the label you gave me when you were feeling for the idea around intentions, and working with intentions, that is trying to come through you.

Me: Should I call you something else?

II: No, I quite like "The Intention Idea" – and my initials I.I. ☺ Let's leave it at that and stay open to where we go together.

Me: You don't know where we're going together?

II: Nope. It's a co-creation. Every idea and intention that manifests is a co-creation that varies by the people and ideas involved. It's unpredictable. Like the sea (apparently a very effective metaphor in a lot of instances): it's fluid, changing, and unpredictable. You can feel a general direction, and point in that direction with your actions, but you won't really know the outcome until you get there. How Fun! ☺

DAY 9

Me: It's New Year's Eve and tomorrow, New Year's Day, is also a Full Moon. That got me to thinking about how much my energies and intentions can be affected by mass consciousness (there are a lot of people setting intentions for the New Year) — and maybe influenced by astrological events (I hear new moons and full moons are good times to focus on intentions).

Is it good to align with these energetic influences? What if the mass consciousness isn't going in a direction I prefer (like in the case of terrorism, or hate and violence events in society)?

II: Yes, humans are all attuned to effects in mass consciousness and planetary / Universe goings-on. Some are more aware of their attunement than others and, therefore, more aware of feeling affected. I feel it's good to be aware of these effects, with the caveat to *not* feel limited by them.

Here's what I mean, and I'll use the flock of birds analogy again...

When you are aware of how the flock as a whole is feeling, or what the entire flock is experiencing in any moment, you can decide to tap into that experience, to lend more energy to the relevant intentions. Here I mean both the flock's intentions and your individual intentions that are in alignment with the flock. If the flock's focus of attention is *not* in alignment with your intentions, it may be a good time to fly solo, or to sit and wait for a more opportune time to bring the flock's attention to your intentions.

At these times of mis-alignment, or non-alignment, it is best to be OK with what-is. Find an intention you have that *can* align with what-is — like an opportunity to increase your compassion for others, or to take a break from pushing (hint, hint), or to nourish yourself so you have more energy for creating on another day. Or, even better, use this as an opportunity to remove and release some of *your* limiting beliefs and feelings that could be related to the direction of the flock/Universe that you are not enjoying or desiring.

The Universe is always in a flow of energies, and that includes mass consciousness. When you align your intentions with this flow in some way – not making your intentions the *same*, but finding a way to *relate* your intentions to the current Universal energy and directional exploration – then your intentions will have access to greater Power supporting them, and less interference blocking them.

Me: So if I feel mysteriously blocked, or low energy, should I check in on what's happening in mass consciousness and/or the planets?

II: You can, but do not make it a rule to follow. The most important thing is that you stay in your heart and *Feel* what your next step is for the intentions you are holding.

How you feel and sense your directions may be different and change for each person, and in each moment, so focus more on your intuitive feelings of what to do, rather than any logical mind reasonings.

Me: Are moons really good times for focusing on intentions? Why?

II: They can be. The nice thing about moon intentions is that the moon has a regular ebb and flow, reminding you to release limitations as well as create intentions. I expect that aligning with the moon phases will help you keep from trying to push the river. That's definitely a good thing!

DAY 10

Me: When is it important to speak an intention out loud and share it with others, versus when to keep it to myself?

II: Be careful of making rules about this. ☺ It's OK for you to wonder and question how things work, but if you turn my answers into rules (instead of guidelines, or just another perspective), then you are limiting and constraining your ability to create. If I *were* going to give you a rule, it would be to lighten up! ☺

So, yes, sometimes it feels better to keep an intention to yourself – not shared with others, not verbally spoken, but internally felt and a driving force for how you are directing your attention. Really, no intention is truly "kept to yourself" because every intention is having an impact on mass consciousness and the sea of intentions. You're just used to being around most people who have not finely tuned their awareness senses to be able to feel your intentions. Or, if they do sense your intention, your society calls them crazy, or weird, or wrong, since what they are sensing is invisible and can be lied about when confronted. Not that you would ever have done that as a human – lied about what you were truly intending. ☺

Anyway, yes, not speaking your intentions, and even deliberately not sharing them, is helpful when you are intending things in daily life. For example, it's awkward to announce every next action you will take. "I'm going to stand up and get a cup of tea now." "I'm going to let the dog outside." "I'm going to go shopping and get some awesome new clothes." You are used to holding daily intentions in your mind, non-verbally, and acting on them. This is a good thing. It may be helpful to speak your intentions out loud if you are unsure of them, or if you want to uncover limiting beliefs or feelings of doubt that hold you back from creating the intention. Many people use affirmations as intentions in this spoken-word way. Speaking your intention does not make it more powerful, but sometimes you put more power into things you have decided to voice.

And also, sharing your intentions with another person *who you trust* can help you explore perspectives on how to manifest your intention, as well as add more power to your intention – as long as they are aligned with it too. If they disagree with it, then you have some work to do to clear up the limiting beliefs and contradicting feelings in *your* space that they are manifesting and mirroring for you.

Me: This makes it feel like I'm always intending *something*, even if I don't say it out loud?

II: Pretty much / Almost. Sometimes you are coasting on past intentions. But most often you are deciding what you want to create to experience next. Sometimes you have a lot of smooth sailing in creating your desired experiences – very few impeding waves from other intentions and a complete alignment with Universal Flow.

And sometimes you experience choppy waters, where it seems you are tossed about and not moving in any desirable directions of experience. That's a good indicator that it's time to investigate underlying intentions you have that you did not realize were still in place.

DAY 11

Me: You mentioned choppy waters of my intentions and (seemingly) other people's intentions colliding with my current intention. What are ways of navigating these waters and making them smoother?

II: As I have said before – check that your intention has alignment with the Universal Flow. If it doesn't, either get it aligned or let it go for now. (Sometimes you will find the Universe flowing in that direction at a later or different time.)

If it is in alignment, and you are still experiencing choppy waters, then it's time to explore impeding intentions. If it's your own impeding intention, usually becoming aware of the actual impeding intention is enough for you to automatically turn off your energy toward that impeding intention. It's usually enough to trigger the "off-switch" because your current intention is so important to you. Like if you were leaving your house and noticed a burner was on, of course you would turn it off.

Me: What if I am aware of an impeding intention, but I can't seem to turn it off? Like an addiction – I am aware the addiction isn't good for my health intentions, but I can't seem to stop it?

II: Yes, addictive behaviors are their own unique territory. Usually you haven't stopped an addictive-like intention, because you really haven't found the underlying intention that the addictive behavior is covering up. Like a person with migraines who keeps getting them because of an underlying, hidden intention to have time at home alone. Once you really, honestly see the real underlying impeding intention, then you can more easily choose to turn it off – from a position of power rather than out of resistance.

Me: How does someone find the impeding intention?

II: It depends on the person and the resources they have available — and their willingness to explore their consciousness honestly.

For you, you have the Avatar tools which are ideal for uncovering and turning off impeding intentions. Other people might use belief work tools like EFT, NLP, talk therapies, or any other forms of exploration and control of specific beliefs and mind stuff.

Me: So, use whatever you have and go looking for impediments to the current intention?

II: In a nutshell, yes. When you are openly, honestly looking for what may be impeding you — not looking out of fear or resistance — but really looking from a place of loving curiosity and appreciation for what-is, then you can more easily see and find the hidden obstacles, and integrate what you need from each one.

Most people would rather just keep all their attention focused on the new intention and hope for the best, but your willingness to see and experience *everything* as it is will bring greater fluidity and alignment with the Flow of the Universe.

It's like driving a car: it's great to have your foot on the gas pedal with all your energy put toward where you want to go. But if you aren't willing to notice if your foot is also on the brake, then you are in for a choppy ride.

DAY 12

Me: What happens if I have too many intentions I want to create? Does it slow down the manifestation of all of them? Is it better to have a short list of prioritized intentions? Or should I hold intentions for absolutely every area of my life?

II: That's a lot of questions. Let me pull it apart for you. Let's take the driving analogy and roll with it for a while. Say you're driving your car and you know where you're going. That's your overall intention, and you put your foot on the gas to supply Power to your intention and make it happen. You are also aware of other drivers on the road, and you harmonize with them and the Flow of traffic so that everyone can gracefully get to their intended destinations.

Now say you want to make a few stops on the way to your destination – like errand running around town, or sight-seeing while on a long road trip. These intentional stops delay the manifestation of your original intention, but at the same time they are also important to you to manifest. Sometimes these additional "intention-stops" even inform your next steps toward your first directional intention. And, they can be just as enjoyable and valuable as the journey you started on toward your first intention.

See? No judgment of additional intentions – only appreciation and incorporation of them. And if you follow this analogy for how it feels to run errands in town, sometimes your multiple intentions will line up near each other and it's super easy to achieve a couple of intentions together by heading in a certain direction. And sometimes your intentions are in opposite directions, so you get to decide which one to go after first. Of course, whichever one you go after first may still pave the way for the intention that appears to be in the opposite direction – you never know what magical opportunities may appear once you start moving in a direction toward your intention. The Universe has a way of facilitating harmony, alignment, and things just working out.

As for your question about lists of intentions – this is just *one* way you can work with them. If you like lists, or affirmations, or dream/vision boards, or goals, then do them. Just know that you can (and are) creating intentions daily with your thoughts. Writing intentions down can help you and your mind have clarity over what you are intending. But, having a list of intentions doesn't make it so. It's when you direct your attention to your intentions, apply some Universal energy and Power to them, Feel them, and take some action, that your intentions really start to take form. Don't sit in your car idly dreaming – take it out for a drive! ☺

DAY 13

Me: What can I do when I have a lot of ideas that want to manifest through me? I feel bad when I don't get to them all. Do you have any suggestions on how to handle prioritizing the many wonderful ideas that I think about creating?

II: It's great that you are tapped into the Universal Flow of ideas and can hear and receive them. But just because you can receive an idea, doesn't mean you should be the one to manifest it. Ideas are looking for a good fit – the right person or persons, at the right time or times, in order to have the intended impact upon manifestation.

Try thinking of all the many wonderful ideas coming to you as if it were a menu. You don't want to eat everything on the menu at one sitting – that would be uncomfortable and unpleasant, and all the ideas couldn't be savored and appreciated that way. Instead you order one or two items you feel most like enjoying now.

It's possible that some ideas on the menu of possibilities won't be on the menu the next time you tune in and look at the menu. That's OK. They might come back some other time, or they might be manifested/manifesting through someone else. Your job is *not* to manifest *all* the ideas that come to you. But hopefully you will stick with it and keep showing up for those ideas that you have promised energy to in some way or form.

Me: How do I promise energy to an idea or intention?

II: It's an energetic contract – you decide you will do it, and that gets the ball rolling.

Me: What happens if I change my mind and decide not to pursue an idea or intention?

II: Then you don't do it, and the idea moves on. It's when you don't decide, but stay unclear, undecided, or cross-committed, that you experience the choppy waters scenario on your intention sea. If you will clearly decide "Not Now," or "No, not for me," instead of keeping an idea or intention on your list in a limbo state of "I don't know," then you won't experience so much drama and trauma over the many wonderful ideas knocking at your door.

Me: It seems like ideas I have had in the past sometimes come into my awareness again when someone else has manifested it. Like yesterday, when I saw the video about crows being trained to pick up cigarette butt trash in exchange for food. It reminded me of the idea I had as a kid to train seagulls to pick up trash off the beaches. Why does that happen sometimes, where I see my idea manifested in some other way?

II: It's awesome, isn't it? The World of Consciousness is so connected, and you can see that more clearly when these instances of ideas-manifested-through-other-channels appear. You could think of it like the idea sending you a wink, or waving hello, to let you know it made it into the manifested world. Like it's saying "Hey, everything's alright! Look, I made it!"

It could be comforting to you, to realize ideas and intentions will keep working to find their way into the physical realms, so maybe you can relax further and not feel responsible for *all* of them.

Me: Yes, that helps. It feels like what Liz Gilbert says in *Big Magic* – to be gracious in my responses and conversations with ideas, even when declining an offer to work on manifesting one. I can still wish each idea well on its way to manifestation – wish that it finds the perfect manifestation resources with perfect timing.

II: And so it will. ☺

DAY 14

Me: You've been using the terms ideas and intentions together lately – are they the same?

II: No, just related. As we talk about the ideas that you become aware of (on your menu of ideas you could choose to manifest), I thought it would be helpful for you to see the connection with your intentions.

Once you *decide* to work on helping an idea to manifest, you are now using your intention to make it happen.

It's part of what an idea needs in order to manifest – human intention to bring it into the physical realm. Without that intention, and usually some human action, the idea will keep floating in the quantum soup as an idea.

Me: So, my intention is a key ingredient for making things manifest into the physical realm?

II: Absodarnlutely! And other realms besides physical too. If you want something to happen – to have any kind of movement or result – it starts with the idea turned into an intention.

Me: Is that what you are now? An idea turned into an intention?

II: I'm on my way. And your name for me fits – I'm the Intention Idea. The Idea about Intentions whose final or fully realized form isn't fully clear yet. But each time you hold your decision/promise to pay attention to me, you help me manifest further. It's like pregnancy – you don't know yet what I'll look like when I'm born, but you're committed to my continued development. Thank you! ☺

THE INTENTION IDEA

Me: My pleasure. ☺

DAY 15

Me: This last year of focusing on creating my intentions, I became very aware of a tendency to try to "push the river." I feel I integrated a lot around that theme, so that I'm not trying to control and force something to work out the way I think it should. I've become more aware of, and aligned with, the flow of the Universe while I'm creating my intentions. But today at work, I watched my colleagues pushing the river and really whipping themselves and those around them into a frenzy, with only a little movement forward and a whole lot of reactive energy. (It's not so pleasant to be around or work with – I prefer a calmer, decision-oriented work space.) Anyway, the contrast got me wondering why some of us humans like to push the river, when it clearly doesn't create that great of results. What's your perspective on this?

II: What you say is true in the realms I play in. "Pushing the river," or otherwise trying to control and force an outcome, is not nearly as effective (or as pleasant) as working in harmony with the Divine / The Universe to co-create a best-fit outcome.

Why humans tend toward force and control, over relaxed intention and power, probably has to do with the mind. I mean, the beliefs and indoctrinations that have conditioned the mind to go first toward force and control. You can see a lot of the indoctrinations in your society about pushing to be number one, be a winner, pulling yourself up by the bootstraps, and not taking "no" for an answer. There's an implied attitude that the person who pushes or pulls the hardest and the most will win and get their way. And with that attitude is the corresponding expectation that yielding, allowing, or working with an existing flow will make you a loser who sacrifices, compromises, or otherwise doesn't get what they really want.

Me: Yep, those ideas, attitudes, and thoughts feel very familiar and very real.

II: Well, they aren't any more real than any other idea or thought — it just depends on how much energy you put into them.

Me: With the way you described pushing the river as "force and control," it makes sense that it would feel choppy and resistant in a sea of harmonious intentions. But say more please, about why force and control isn't as effective, and what beliefs or ideas can I hold to foster more alignment and co-creating with the Universal Flow?

II: Well, you get it in a feeling sense, why force and control doesn't work well in a space of harmony. Here's another analogy to bring it home:

Say you're playing in an orchestra, and you have all rehearsed together and know your parts and your timing to make a sound that is the most pleasing to everyone — the players and the audience. Force and Control approaches are like, if a specific instrument player came in off-beat, out of tune, too loudly, or even in a totally different key or song. It interrupts the whole effect. Sure, the individual using control and force will be heard, but that doesn't mean that the whole orchestra is now playing their tune. It's a partial victory — and really a pretty small one.

Now, if you are looking at your intentions as part of a creative whole — like an instrument player in an orchestra — then you can more easily find beliefs that feel good to you and support that goal.

Me: Will you give me some examples of beliefs?

II: OK, but please don't get attached to them. When talking about beliefs it's really important that you see the art of keeping them flexible, and changing them as you need to for what you want to experience next.

Me: OK, I'll take your belief suggestions as ideas — not laws.

THE INTENTION IDEA

II: Perfect! Here are a couple of ideas and thoughts that, if you hold them as beliefs with strong conviction, can help you align even more with a relaxed Intention and Power approach (rather than Control and Force):

Everything is All Right.
Everybody Wins.
The journey and who I become is just as important as the end result.
There's always a way to do things harmoniously.
Everything I do aligns with and benefits all of humanity.
We are all in this together.
OK to that. OK to that too.
We can do this.
Things always work out for the best for everyone.
I am a co-creator.
We go farther and further when we work together.
We are an aligned team.
It's all good.
We are all going to get there.
We are doing it!
Everything in Perfect Timing for the Highest Benefit of All.
Ease and Grace wins the race.

DAY 16

Me: We use a lot of different terms around the topic of creating intentions and I'm wondering if you can help break down the distinctions between them, and how they work together? I'm specifically interested in these concepts as they relate to creating an intention:
- vision
- visualization
- confidence
- self-esteem
- belief
- thought
- idea

II: You are feeling very logic-minded as you ask this question and look at this list. I suppose that is what can happen when a mind tries to understand what is happening in the unseen realms of the quantum soup – it tries to bring order by sorting, labeling, defining, and organizing.

Me: Should I not be taking a logical approach to understanding how to work better at creating my intentions?

II: It's OK, I just want to remind you to also stay flexible and fluid in your approach to life and creating your experiences. If you harden things into rules, you start to limit your possibilities for further explorations.

Me: OK, duly noted. If I take your responses to my questions as perspectives, rather than rules or laws, will you please share with me your current perspective on the distinctions between these terms / ideas we have for working with intentions?

II: Yes, gladly. And thank you for recognizing that these are my *current* perspectives — things can change, perspectives can change, ideas can change. That's the beauty of co-creation — we all keep learning and growing with each other.

Me: So how about vision and visualization first? What's your perspective on these concepts as they relate to creating intentions?

II: I love vision and visualization. Both of these ways of using your attention can be very helpful in creating an intention. Humans often think of a vision as being similar to an intention. When you work with vision boards you are solidifying, clarifying, or otherwise bringing more senses like sight, sound, feeling, and words to your intentions.

It's probably good for you to distinguish between your intention — your direction of energy toward a perceived outcome — and these tools you use to help you make it more real, palpable, and relatable in your physical realm or to your other senses. How you use vision and visualization can determine if it's supportive of your intention energy, or if it's constraining or limiting the possibilities in some way. What I mean is, if you create a vision with pictures and/or words, or you use some form of visualization where you are imagining your intention realized — playing it like a movie in your mind — then you could be confining yourself to *only that* picture, that *one* way of having your intention realized. If you want your intention to manifest with the most ease and grace, in harmony with the Universe, then you will be best served by keeping your visions and visualizations open, fluid, flexible, and more focused on the general feel of your intention than a detailed, specific outcome.

Me: That makes me think of the phrase I learned from Marc Allen's books about manifesting.

II: Yes! Just like Marc Allen uses as his caveat phrase on any vision / intention:

THE INTENTION IDEA

> "This or something better is coming to me now
> with ease and grace and perfect timing
> for the benefit of ALL."

This is a great way to keep your mind open to possibilities it would not otherwise see, or recognize, if it is locked in on a vision. Imagine having tunnel vision where all you can see is one option at the end of a tunnel, versus having a widened-back, expansive view of the entire horizon. You can see how, in the latter option, you will be more open to seeing and taking other paths that may get you to your desired outcome more easily. Or, taking a widened-back view of your vision may even inform your vision with new ideas that enrich your experience. You would not be able to take part in those new ideas if you are committed to the "tunnel vision path."

Me: Do you have any suggestions for how to use vision and visualization more effectively, like in this widened-back approach?

II: Well, it is helpful to give your mind and your senses something to chew on, and visions and visualization are ways of directing your attention toward your intentions. Perhaps you could start by creating many varieties of your vision or visualization. That could keep your mind from creating a rut of always seeing your vision or doing your visualization the same way.

Anything that helps you interact with your vision or visualization from a place of curiosity, wonder, and exploration will help you stay open to the possibilities during the process of creating your intention.

Me: This feels like how my daily video blog worked for me last year. I put my attention on a topic for a short amount of time each day, talked about it, and changed themes of exploration each month. There was a lot of discovery for me just in talking it out.

II: Yes, your video blog was a good example of how to do this. You put your attention on your intention every day in a light mood of exploration. You looked for additional perspectives on your intention and enjoyed the journey of seeing how themes in consciousness connected together for a better understanding and integration of the whole.

It seems that humans often set a vision – like goals at the New Year – and then let it sit like a ruler written in stone: the vision isn't allowed to change, and you measure yourself against it. This is not a very effective or kind way to work with visions, or to manifest an intention. Keeping your attention light, playful, curious, and exploratory will help you to manifest.

Remember that we are all playing and co-creating together, so flexibility helps us to create intentions harmoniously. And rules, single-minded thinking, and seriousness make it much more challenging to manifest … I mean the un-fun kind of challenging.

DAY 17

Me: My qigong instructor talks about acting with intention being like acting with confidence. If you doubt that you are interacting with the energy the way you intended, then the movements are not as powerful as when you act with confidence that your intention is so – that it is occurring. I'd love your perspectives on confidence as it relates to intention. Also, if or how self-esteem relates. Self-esteem seems similar to confidence – or maybe a necessary ingredient in order to act with confidence?

II: What you are learning in your qigong practice is very valuable practice for working with the unseen energies of intention, and trusting your senses that something is indeed happening when you energize your intention. And yes, acting with confidence, and holding your intention with confidence, are very valuable ways of working with intention.

Let's go back to the ocean wave analogy, to further explore how confidence and intention work together. If you recall, in this analogy your intention is like a wave heading for shore, and reaching the shore is when your intention has fully manifested in the physical realms. So now imagine you are initiating this wave with a push of your hand. How much Universal Energy you are tapped into will determine how much power is put into the movement of the wave. But if you don't also act with confidence as you direct the Universal Energy, then the slap of your hand on the water may not have much clear direction, or maybe not much effect. You may end up patting the water instead of giving it a clear push. You can see how not acting with confidence could make your intention sea choppy again – or just stagnant.

Me: Indeed. And what about self-esteem? How does that factor in?

II: Humans get pretty funny around this term. It's used often as a measurement, a badge of honor, a stick to beat yourself with, and even as a limitation – like a rope on a swimming pool keeping you from going in the deep end of "too much self-esteem." If you were to go back to the roots of this word, it's really much more about how you regard your "self," what you believe about yourself. It's not really about your ego, or positive thinking, or feeling good about yourself. All of those things are a result of what you believe about yourself, and whether that collage of beliefs has a net impact of helping you feel good, or not so good.

Me: From this perspective that self-esteem is really my beliefs about myself, how does it relate to confidence and intention? Or does it?

II: Yes it does, because all of your beliefs – whether about yourself, your intentions, or your world – all of them impact your experiences and therefore impact your ability to create your intentions.

Let's say your collage of beliefs about yourself leads you toward feeling unworthy or undeserving of good results unless you work really hard to prove yourself. Some people might label you as having low self-esteem because of that belief. Regardless of the label, the effect of the belief is that your confidence and flow toward creating your intentions occurs only if you feel you are working hard and overcoming challenges, in order to prove that you have earned and now deserve the good outcome of your realized intention. In other words, with this particular type of self-belief in place, you will not be able to confidently hold your intention and manifest it with complete ease and grace. There has to be some struggle and hard work involved first.

The effect of this self-belief is a limitation on how your intention can manifest. That's not to say that it won't still manifest, but your belief is forcing it into that tunnel-vision, only-one-way type of path, rather than allowing a broad expansive view on a sea of possibilities.

Me: What if I believe that I am valuable, worthy, and deserving of ease and grace?

II: Then that is what you will experience. And just like the previous example, you could be labeled according to your self-esteem, but focusing on the label of low or high self-esteem doesn't really determine the outcome of your experiences. It's really the detailed beliefs you have about yourself, and about your ability to create your intentions, that will have the unique effects on your manifestation journey.

DAY 18

Me: Our last conversation feels like a perfect segue to hear your perspectives on beliefs, thoughts, and ideas and how they relate to intentions. Care to elaborate and share?

II: As you might suspect from our conversation so far, beliefs play a very important role in your ability to create your intentions. If you think of beliefs like colored glasses, or even glasses with different magnifications, you can see how each unique belief can impact your perception and your interpretation of your experiences. And having a collage of beliefs, as all humans do, compounds that influence on your perceptions and experiences even more as your beliefs collide, amplify, counter each other, or otherwise interact. Then add in other people's beliefs, and the overall swell of beliefs in mass consciousness, and you can feel how there are, or can be, *many* influences on your state of mind, attitude, perceptions of what's possible, and interpretations of what-is.

Me: Sounds like a tangled web that would be difficult to navigate or sort out.

II: Yes, it is complex, but with the right tools and an exploratory attitude it's not *that* difficult to navigate. It's more like an adventure in navigating toward your intended direction. If everything were a fast straight-line to creation, you might get a little bored – and you might create some big things you didn't really want, that take some effort to undo.

Me: Feels like I'm in a training ground for learning how to manifest, so I'll be able to handle bigger and bigger intentions and creations as I progress in my abilities.

II: Very much so. Only unlike the concept of a training ground, every intention you create means something valuable to you, and you get to enjoy every aspect of your learning journey.

Me: What are the tools for navigating the tangled web of beliefs, so that I'm only using beliefs that support my intentions and not so swayed or impacted by the limiting beliefs (both mine and other's)?

II: You have the Avatar tools – again an excellent toolkit for navigating both the positive / helpful beliefs you want to install into your mind's operating system and also for finding and plucking out the beliefs that are constraining you in some way.

Much like the bacterial environment of your digestive tract, there's an important balanced approach when working with beliefs. If all you do is wipe out the limiting beliefs – like using antibiotics to kill off the harmful bacteria – then you are very open to a new infestation of beliefs – harmful or helpful. You're a blank slate, but that can also mean you are more open and vulnerable to indoctrinations – from mass consciousness, or peers, or media, or … many sources. You can rebalance by installing new beliefs that you feel will be helpful for your intentions.

And the reverse scenario is also true. If you only focus on adding in positive beliefs – like taking loads of probiotics – then it may help to slowly crowd out the limiting beliefs (bad bacteria), but you may still be impacted by the limiting beliefs that are hanging on. You can rebalance by doing some periodic cleansing in order to *fully* support the beneficial beliefs (good bacteria) you want to help grow.

So you see, a dance or flow that uses both removal of limiting beliefs and an inoculation of helpful beliefs gives you the best environment for fostering and creating your intentions.

Me: If someone doesn't have the Avatar tools what can they use to navigate this dance of removing limiting beliefs and installing helpful beliefs?

II: As long as they are aware of and focused on achieving this dance, they will find the perfect tools for them in that moment. You've heard me mention some options before and I'll remind you of them now.

For removal of limiting beliefs someone could use tools like NLP, EFT, and some types of body work that focus on removing or breaking up old patterns. For installing new beliefs someone could use affirmations, NLP, EFT, and repeated attention on the new belief.

Me: This seems like a short list.

II: These are just a couple of examples. Look for any tools that enable you (and any helpful guide or practitioner) to maintain a lightness of being as you go exploring with beliefs. Use any tool that helps you navigate beliefs without getting caught up in a "right and wrong" way of seeing the beliefs.

Essentially you are working *with* the mind and its structures to co-create an intention. That means you need to be able to investigate and alter the software programming that the mind has running on automatic. When *you* as a Higher Self have mastery over your mind, and how you direct your attention and Universal Energy, then your intention creating is limitless and *Full* of Possibility!

DAY 19

Me: Can we explore these analogies a little more? First you were talking about beliefs like managing the balance of good and bad bacteria in the gut. Now you're talking about managing the mind like it is software programming. How do these analogies work together?

II: First of all, remember that they are analogies. They are meant to inform and expand on a perspective with imagery and existing systems that can parallel the thing we're talking about. Analogies are not a precise or direct comparison. They are useful for helping you to understand, relate to, and integrate concepts that are new to you. But if you try to make an analogy a direct comparison, or relate too many detailed parts to the thing you're trying to understand, then the analogy loses its value.

Me: Is that why you use several different types of analogies?

II: Yes, that, and also because I am working with concepts that are familiar to you – ideas that already have some structure in your mind that are relevant to the new structure we are exploring together.

Me: OK, so as you talk about managing beliefs being like balancing bacteria in the gut, it makes me think about the video I just watched where the doctor said it was important to have a wide variety of good bacteria. He suggested not overloading your system with just one or two types of good bacteria, like you could be doing if you take a lot of probiotics that are millions of units of the same one or two bacteria. Does that part of the analogy apply to managing beliefs, or am I getting too detailed in my comparison?

II: It's good that you checked before assuming that it's exactly the same. That's good use of an analogy. ☺

So, again, I'll point to the value of dancing in the Flow. If you make a hard rule that you should (or should not) hold multiple positive beliefs, then you start to close off the options to do the opposite – or even something in between – as needed.

The more you are in tune with the general concept and *feel* of how intentions and belief management work, the easier it is for you to intuit and navigate how to balance and re-balance in any particular moment, for any specific need.

Perhaps the more important structure for you to pay attention to in this analogy, and what you heard the doctor saying about how ideal gut health works, is that the environment and communication within, across, and AS the whole system is just as important, or more important, than any individual part's role or task.

So, focusing on one bacteria type, or on one belief, is not as valuable to the creation of your intentions as it is to care for the entire environment or collage of your beliefs, how they are all interacting and communicating with each other, and how they are working together to create your experiences.

Me: Is this why you then moved to the analogy of a mind running on software?

II: Yes, partially. Let me expand this analogy so you can better see how it relates and informs your perceptions of beliefs and intentions.

If your mind were like a computer, you would have a basic operating system that gives you an environment from which to create and explore software applications that are unique to your interests. The operating system would handle basic things like perception, communication, operating the body, and maybe even house some core beliefs about who you are, why you're here, and what to do next in your evolutionary path. Beliefs would be more like software applications that you choose to install or uninstall. Those "belief applications" provide experiences unique to each belief. Some you are running in the foreground, deliberately interacting with and focusing on them. Some are running in the background. Some run automatically upon certain triggers, or just all the time. And some are like Trojan horse viruses – you don't know how they got in there, they are running behind the scenes, they are harder to find to turn off or uninstall, and they generally prevent you from running the other belief applications you want to be focusing on.

You can see how, in this analogy, there is a whole environment of beliefs – both helpful and impeding – that are communicating, doing their own thing, and basically contributing to your overall experiences – both of your mind and of your life.

In both the "beliefs as digestive tract bacteria" and the "beliefs as mind software" analogies you can feel the importance of emphasizing a balance toward helpful beliefs, removal of unhelpful beliefs that interfere, and good coordination and communication of the whole system that the beliefs are a part of. When you view beliefs from this holistic perspective of all the moving parts *and* the whole moving forward on an experiential journey, then you have more intuitive understanding of how to work with intentions.

Me: How so?

II: As you manage the beliefs, so also do you manage your intentions, and so also do you have more energy directed holistically toward a common goal.

Me: Are you saying I have a mix of good intentions and bad intentions that need to be managed like beliefs?

II: Labeling intentions "good" or "bad" can trip you up in how you work with intentions. Think of it more as intentions that are aligned with the Universal Flow and the common good, compared to intentions misaligned or even contradicting the Universal Flow, and more self-serving than supporting the common good.

THE INTENTION IDEA

Me: How do I use the belief managing analogies to better manage my intentions?

II: Just like with your beliefs environment, you can also inspect your intentions and keep rebalancing toward more and more intentions that serve the common good, and keep weeding out any intentions that are purely self-serving or going against the harmonious Universal Flow.

Me: I can sense a gardening analogy coming next – you said weeding. ☺ Are there any tools to help rebalance my intentions?

II: Loads of tools! We're going to have fun creating even more as we play together. For starters, focusing on your intentions, writing them down, saying them out loud, taking a walk as you lightly put your attention on them, drawing them, and generally exploring what each intention feels like. We can get into more detailed tools later, but this is a good place to start.

Me: What about tools for weeding out the intentions that are out of alignment with the Universal Flow and common good?

II: Loads of tools for that too, and especially your Avatar tools. Let's finish your question about beliefs, ideas, and thoughts first.

Me: You could feel my mind still niggling about that unfinished thread, huh?

II: Very prominently in the way of our next step together. ☺

Me: OK, to close the loop on this topic, the remaining question I have is how ideas and thoughts relate to intentions. You talked a lot about beliefs, but how do thoughts and ideas relate to creating intentions?

THE INTENTION IDEA

II: From my perspective, thoughts are a potential seed of an idea, belief, or intention. If you sit and observe your mind's thoughts, you'll see a whole variety of things pass by. Some can feel random, and some will be related to whatever is drawing your attention right now – whether from perceptions of your physical environment, or from repeated cycles of attention on topics in your mind space. And some thoughts will be deliberate – you are actively choosing to think about something in the present moment.

Sometimes a thought will come into your mind space and you will decide to make it very important. You may even decide, "this is the way it is." Once you've made that decision, you've turned the passing thought into a belief. It could be a strongly held belief with a lot of conviction in it, or it may be lightly held with more flexibility for it to change. Either way, once you've decided that "this is the way it is" at any level – maybe not deliberately or consciously – then you start to shape your perceptions and experiences according to how that belief affects and adds to your overall belief collage.

Me: You've used that term "belief collage" several times. Can you explain it a little more so it's clear?

II: You know what a collage looks like: lots of photos and words, often overlapping each other, designed to give an overall experience – like the overall feel of a vision board – but still with all the individual parts being something you can focus on and interpret in some way. Your collection of beliefs is like a collage: you can see and inspect the individual beliefs if you focus on them, but generally as you move through life, you are operating from the foundation of all your beliefs put together – all of them glued to you until you choose to peel some off.

Me: Makes sense. So, if a thought once strengthened by my decision "this is the way it is" becomes a belief, when does a thought become an idea or intention?

II: Idea is a term that can get confused often. Maybe because it has an element of possession – whose idea is it? Somehow that importance of possession seems to add a layer of confusion about ideas for the human mind. From my perspective, ideas are thoughts outside of the mind looking for expression. When a mind (or a heart) connects with an idea, there's an opportunity for co-creation and manifestation of the idea.

When humans talk about "coming up with an idea," or "having an idea," they most often are referring to the concept of using the mind to think about something and form an idea all on their own. Artists are more likely to understand the concept of an idea being separate from you and co-creating with the human mind. This is because most artists are more tapped in to the Universal Flow and the concept that they are working with a muse, or an energy, that isn't all them, their mind, or their skills.

Me: Your description sounds a lot like what Elizabeth Gilbert proposed in *Big Magic* – that ideas exist separately from humans.

II: Yes, I very much like Liz Gilbert's presumption that ideas roam the earth in search of a good match with a human who will help to co-create and manifest them.

Me: So, ideas have more energy than thoughts?

II: You could say that. You notice how, when you receive and perceive an idea, you often have that energetic rush of an aha! feeling? That is the effect of you connecting with this energy that is new to you. I would say it often seems "outside" of you, but from the perspective that we are all one, there is no outside. Let's just say that the idea is outside of the current structures of your mind, so it causes a little restructuring of what you thought you knew.

Me: How do each of these terms now relate to intentions?

II: Well, thoughts pass along and sometimes become beliefs by your decision that "this is the way it is." Once it's a belief it's part of the belief collage that impacts how you perceive and experience. That means it can impact your ability to perceive and receive ideas and your ability to create your intentions.

Me: I get it. And how is an idea different than an intention?

II: Intentions are a human thing – at least in the context we're talking about now – they aren't disembodied like ideas can be. A human can interact with an idea and make an intention out of it by deciding "I'm going to …" whatever the action of the idea is.

Me: It seems like thoughts are to beliefs what ideas are to intentions – seeds that, when decided upon, can turn into the more solidified belief or intention?

II: Almost. Solidified isn't quite the right word to describe beliefs or intentions, because both beliefs and intentions can be quite flexible in their forms. A better description might be that beliefs and intentions are like the fruits of the seeds. In fact, go with this analogy and you can see that your decision is what catalyzes the seed and gets it to begin germinating. As it grows it can eventually manifest into a fruit that bears more seeds.

Me: That seems a little confusing. Can you clarify or use a different analogy?

II: OK. Imagine your thought, or an idea, floating around out there like dandelion seeds on the wind. Your human mind-heart-will environment is the soil where this thought or idea could land. If it lands and is a good fit for your specific mind-heart-will terrain, then it's likely to take hold. Your decision to keep it there, water it, and foster its growth is the catalyst that turns that thought or idea into a belief or intention. And just because you've decided to support its growth, that doesn't mean it is now immediately manifested as a new dandelion plant or flower. You may need to take additional actions,

THE INTENTION IDEA

or simply keep nurturing the belief or intention until you have a physical manifestation of it. Nevertheless, as soon as you have decided to let it grow in your mind-heart-will environment, it is actively taking root as part of your belief collage or intention sea, and it is having an impact on your life experience.

Me: That seems both cool and scary.

II: It's only scary if you think about all the non-deliberate, automatic, or unconscious decisions you make to let thoughts and ideas stay in your space. The good news is that you have the ability to weed out anything that is taking root that you feel no longer serves you. And, you can deliberately seek and find new thoughts and ideas you would prefer to plant and grow – you don't have to wait for a favorable wind. ✋

DAY 20

Me: I've started typing our conversations so that it's easier to share with people. Do you have any preferences or suggestions on how I share it, or with whom?

II: I trust your intuition on who to share it with. I'm talking with you with the intention that our conversation, and the perspectives within it, can and will be shared with a wide and varied audience.

Me: Do you have a suggestion for how to preface this written form of our interactions?

II: Again, I trust you to feel what will work best to help people understand the basis of our conversations. But also, keep in mind that people will interpret and integrate the information we share from their own belief collages. Some will allow their mental landscape to undergo restructuring, and some won't. That's OK. Our co-creation is to offer the information without restriction or judgment on how it is used.

Me: Shouldn't we care about how the information is used? Like to make sure it isn't distorted into a meaning you didn't intend?

II: *You* can watch for that, but my role as the Intention Idea is to put the ideas out there and trust they will come to fruition one way or another. Outside of a time-based view, it doesn't matter that there may or may not be dips and tangents and sideways swipes while on the path toward our co-creation – it's *all* a part of the journey.

Me: Hmm, being oriented in time, it's harder for me to be OK with such potential distractions, delays, and deterrents to our co-creation manifesting.

THE INTENTION IDEA

II: This is why I say *you* can watch for those deterrents and remedy them if they occur. My interest and attention is only on the co-creation, not on protecting it. The more Universal Power we put into the co-creation, the less chance or concern there is for deterrents.

Me: So, full steam ahead, damn the torpedoes?

II: For me, yes. For you, I suggest dodging the torpedoes if you can, but make sure you are still full steam ahead with me.

Me: Makes me think of the failure video I watched last night. It talked about the value of failing often in order to learn and grow – not holding back, but continuing to practice, practice, practice.

II: Yes, very much like that. You might create scenarios for yourself where you feel safe to practice, and fail, and learn. Like your decision to first share our conversations only with a small group of people you trust. But don't stop there, and always keep going forward, both in your practice and in your expansion of the environments in which you practice (a.k.a. take action).

Me: Baby steps, baby steps …

II: At first, but not forever. At some points you will also take leaps of faith. The point is, keep going forward, no matter what. No matter what responses you get when you share our conversations, no matter how our information is interpreted. Keep going forward with the Bigger Picture of our co-creation in your heart.

DAY 21

Me: One more question about intentions before we go exploring and co-creating tools for working with intentions.

II: OK. You know I'm itching to move toward tools, but also always happy to answer questions and offer and explore perspectives.

Me: Thank you. So, one of the areas around intentions where I know I've gotten hung up, and I've seen others challenged by this too, is with respect to intentions to promote, coerce, or manipulate. Essentially, I can start with a helpful intention – like to share with other people something that I view as beneficial – but then I go down this slippery slope of wanting them to like and use what I've offered. It's particularly noticeable when money is involved, like in a business exchange. When I want to receive money in any way related to what I'm offering, it's like it triggers my "push the river" theme in my consciousness. And then I often feel like promoting, coercing, and manipulating people is OK in order to reach my intended goal. It's not always a conscious, deliberate intention to do whatever it takes like this – in fact I think it's usually pretty hidden … but still felt at some level.

How do I keep my work with intentions from going down this path, especially when manifesting the intention relies on physical support from other people?

II: Yes, this *is* a sticky wicket of Intention Work. I'm glad you brought it up because it is very prevalent in your society right now. It's also damaging, at times, to your ability to work harmoniously and in integrity with *all* of your intentions. Once you start promoting, coercing, manipulating, or in any other form trying to push someone else (or the Universe) into giving you what you want, then you are operating from a self-centered mindset, rather than from a place of contributing to the greater good.

THE INTENTION IDEA

It's historically been a challenging feat for humans to drop the self-centered mindset and operate more altruistically – more in alignment with and in support of the Whole System. It can be done though, especially with practice and focus.

Me: Is this one of those areas where I'm going to have to plan to fail?

II: Indeed. And my suggestion is that you be compassionate with yourself (and with others!) when you notice this behavior of self-centered intention-work. Sometimes people need to establish more of a foundation that "everything is all right" before they can see and operate from the Bigger Picture that "we are all in this together."

Me: Sounds like two really good intentions or beliefs to hold.

II: Yes! Saying these phrases to yourself, or out loud, can help you to establish a firmer foundation of the concept of You in and of the Universe.

Me: What do you mean by "in and of the Universe"?

II: When you are aware of your self-viewpoint in the context that you are *in* the Universe – you live within this greater system – and you are *of* the Universe – your viewpoint is an expression of (or from) this greater system – then you can more easily hold a perspective that is bigger than you while still operating in the world as you. It's easier from this perspective to care for and align with the greater good of the whole system because you don't see yourself as separate from it.

Me: You make it sound simple and easy. Is that all I need to do to keep from misusing my intention – hold the viewpoint of being in and of the Universe?

THE INTENTION IDEA

II: Easy and simple to say, yes. But the human experience is rife with complexity and distractions. So, holding that perspective throughout daily life – and especially when tempted to "get rich quick," or have your intention realized immediately – that is where your practice is, and your compassion and growth through failures.

Me: Can you give me an example of what it would look like to hold the "Whole System" perspective while working with intentions that have to do with receiving money?

II: Sure. Let's say you have an intention to earn a specific amount of money for whatever purpose. I use the word "earn" because that will immediately point you toward a mindset of providing value to others in order to receive your money. If you focus on creating, manifesting, or just receiving money, then you are more prone to misalignment with the Universe. That's not to say you can't or shouldn't ever receive money without "earning it," but it's another slippery slope if you continually want to receive without giving in some way.

So, you have an intention to earn some money, and you have ideas of what you would like to offer the world in exchange for that money. If you keep holding that Bigger Picture Intention with a flexible attitude, and the willingness to keep taking actions as soon as opportunities present themselves, then you *will* eventually manifest the money, and most likely through the offering you have given to the world.

You are most likely to get hung up if you are invested in this manifestation happening in a specific timeframe, or if you are rigid in your expectations of what your offering should look like.

Me: Yes, that sounds familiar – getting attached to having money by a certain date, and attached to my ideas of what my offering should look like and how I think it should be received.

How can I best stay flexible with timing and the services I am offering, so that I don't get caught trying to push again?

II: First of all, remember to be compassionate with yourself when you do push. Being human has a lot of pressures since you are oriented by time as well as many other societal beliefs and expectations. It's OK that you push now and then, and pushing *with* the Universal Flow can be a good thing. It's like pushing someone on a swing to help them go higher. Just try to avoid pushing them when they are coming back the other way. ☺

Second, your awareness of the tendency to push, or be rigid in your expectations, will help you to catch it and stop it when it happens.

And lastly, this is a good segue for us to start talking about tools for working with intentions, because using tools can help you achieve even more flexibility in your viewpoints and approaches to manifesting your intentions.

Me: Oh Boy – tools!

II: Exactly! ☺

PART 2
TOOLS

DAY 22

Me: Let's talk tools. What are tools you suggest for working with and manifesting intentions?

II: Well, let's break this down into several phases so it's easiest for you to digest. First, there are tools to help you come up with an intention in the first place.

Then there are tools for helping you to get a full sense of your intention and really feel the direction of it – like creating a compass that always points you in the right direction for that intention.

Then there are tools for that swampy, in-between time, from when you decide on the intention to when it starts to physically manifest. These are tools for persistence, Faith, removing obstacles, and feeling for next steps.

Then there are tools for the phase of birthing the intention into reality. Like tools for keeping out of egotistical pride and staying connected to the Bigger Picture.

And finally, there are tools for integrating, experiencing, enjoying, and expanding from the physical manifestation, which can often inspire a new wave of intentions.

Me: I'm glad you broke it down like this – it feels like there's a lot more to working with intention than just holding a thought in your mind.

II: Yes, it's good for you to see that there can be phases to the manifestation of an intention, so you don't give up simply because the tools you were using from a previous phase aren't working so well for the phase of manifestation you are at now.

THE INTENTION IDEA

And, once you are aware of the possible phases and tools, you can also choose to work very intuitively with *all* of the tools based on what feels good to you in the moment. You can even make up new tools that work for you. The purpose of these tools is to keep your attention positively focused on your intentions, with enough flexibility to adjust your course, and enough Universal Energy (Power) behind the intentions, to bring them into physical reality. Also, you will develop the ability to intuit what next physical action step to take as part of your human role in the manifestation.

Me: OK, so can we start with "phase 1" – tools for coming up with an intention?

II: OK. These tools are all about helping you to quiet the mind, tune in to the flow of the Universe, listen and feel for what's needed, and imagine / intuit / explore new possibilities beyond what-is, now.

I'm telling you the purpose of the tools so you can also find and create any additional tools that help you achieve this, beyond what I'm going to list out for you now. Stay flexible in your exploration and use of tools – don't turn them into rules. ☺

Here are some tools I am currently aware of that can help you during phase 1:

Meditations – all kinds work, so find one or more that you like. It could be guided, silent, active/walking, static/sitting, directed toward a question, or focused on experiencing exactly what-is. Use your better judgment, or intuition, for what kind of meditation you need in the moment. For example, if you have a very active mind with an overwhelm of ideas, try a quieting meditation form that focuses on achieving stillness. If, in contrast, you feel a bit blank about what to do next or intend next, then try a more active meditation that focuses on creativity, visualization, receiving guidance, or somehow tuning in more to the Universe and the world around you.

Me: Will we create some specific meditations that fit these varied

THE INTENTION IDEA

needs?

II: Maybe. Some and plenty are already in existence – let's just queue up doing a search of what's available first. No need to reinvent the wheel since it's already there, and our time together is better spent first identifying the possibilities to include in our "Intention Work Tool Chest" – or "Toy Chest." ☺

Me: I like the feel of a toy chest – feels like when I was a kid and intentionally pulled out my stuffed animals and other toys, and imagined and played out different scenarios with them.

II: Exactly! Being playful and lighthearted with your intention work is *always* a good thing!

So, in addition to meditations you can also use Creative Arts like writing, drawing, sculpting, singing, painting, finger-painting ☺, doodling, and any kind of relaxed music or dance – one without a very imposed format. When you allow yourself to express whatever is there, in the moment, creatively, then you are automagically tapping into and tuning yourself to the creative energies of the Universe. There is no need to try to direct the creative output – just enjoy tuning into the flow and go wherever it takes you. It's possible that a new intention will come to you during, or immediately after, your creative process. Or, it will at least get you out of your mind, and more into your heart-space, so that you are more receptive to feel new intentions that align with the universal greater good.

Me: Do I have to get out of my analytical mind in order to come up with an aligned intention?

II: No, but it often helps. You can operate your mind *from* your heart-space – and still be able to think with logic – while tuned in to your intuition and the universal flow. This can take some practice though, so it's very helpful for receiving and creating new intentions to use tools that get you out of your overly analytical mind and into your intuitive, connected heart.

THE INTENTION IDEA

Another tool for coming up with an intention is to spend time observing. This is often easiest to do in a place you enjoy, like in nature. If you enjoy being around people for their energy – not out of a place of judgment of them or needing approval from them – then "people-watching" can be another form of observing. Sadly, most people have so many desires and resistances on how other people exist in the world – even strangers! – it's often rare for someone to be able to sustain a relaxed, neutral observation of other people. Nature is a nice, safe place for you to start this practice until you have cleared more of your judgments on others and your desires for approval or attention.

While you are observing, it's OK, and even desirable, to appreciate and enjoy what you are observing. Allow yourself to fully experience whatever is happening right now, and feel the sacredness of your current experience of being alive. Though your society has often praised involvement and participation – and discounted observing and watching – observing is actually a high vibration mode of connecting with the flow of the universe and the pure awareness, background, core part of yourself that always exists. It's not easy to have language for this – some might call it Spirit, or the experience of being One with everything. Thankfully, the words used to describe it are not as important as the actual experience. So, simply start with observing while in nature, and see where that activity takes you in terms of feeling more connected, relaxed in your beingness, and expanded in your awareness.

Lastly for this phase 1 of coming up with intentions, is the tool of playing with words. Words start to move you toward the next phase where you are getting a full sense of your intention. For now, in the context of coming up with an intention, think of words as a rough sketch that helps you feel the differences in an intention focused one way or another. For example, you could start playing with words you like – write them down, draw them, sound them out, and feel how they feel as they come out of your mouth. You may want to do this privately, or with only trusted and informed companions, so that the words you are playing with are not taken as laws or actual intended creations. Let yourself have a playground where you try on the feel

THE INTENTION IDEA

of words, their underlying meanings, and how in different combinations they can point your attention in different directions.

Me: Sounds like a good use of a thesaurus.

II: Could be, but only if you can use it in a creative, light-hearted way. You're not looking for an answer here. You're really just playing with your imagination and intuition, to get a feel for what a new intention might be like to have and to hold, without having to create it yet to have and to hold. ☼

DAY 23

Me: How do you know when you are done with phase 1 and ready for phase 2 of creating an intention?

II: It's better if you don't measure yourself, or your process, by phases – you can too easily get caught up in judgments and lose the light-hearted playfulness of intention work that way. Instead, if you notice that your attention is attracted to a particular intention, allow yourself to explore it more and feel into what its manifestation would be like. Let the feelings of natural excitement, enthusiasm, and joy be your guides as you explore possible intentions. The Universal Flow is always in alignment with expansion of these energies, so you can trust these feelings as a barometer for good things to come from the intention you are exploring.

For tools to help you get a full sense of your intention, you can continue your exploration with words. Only now, you will refine them more into statements, or phrases, that describe what you intend to create. A good place to start is with "I statements," like I am…, I have …, I do …, I create …. I especially like "I create" followed by a short statement of what you are intending to manifest into physical reality.

If you're not yet sure how to describe your intention, you can do more creative art explorations, only now more deliberately focused on exploring the feelings, sensations, big picture, and details of the intention you are interested in. Yes, this is like vision boarding or mind-mapping, where you are connecting all the relevant pieces you are aware of into one bigger picture of the whole intention, and its results on the world (and your life) once manifested.

As you begin to navigate between the energetic realms of intention energy and the physical realms of action and manifestation, then vision boards, mind maps, and intention statements all act as a compass to help re-center on the overall and core energies of your intention.

Me: Once I've created this "intention compass," do I need to revisit it often to make sure I'm on track, or to update or edit it?

II: Well, it's a lot like hiking in the wilderness where there is no trail. You can check your compass direction to get started, and aim for an intermediary milestone or marker that is on the way to the end goal. Once you get to that intermediary milestone, you'll want to check your compass again to find and navigate to the next milestone that you can see in front of you. If there are a lot of obstacles on the path, like big rocks, swamps, lakes, or even mountains between you and the end-goal, then you will check your compass more often than if it is a short, straight line between you and the manifested intention. Checking your compass more often doesn't make your intention manifest faster, but it does help you make sure you are currently on track.

As for updating or editing your intention compass, the only reasons you'd need to do this are if 1) you didn't spend much time contemplating and feeling into the overall direction of your intention in the first place, or 2) you gathered new information while on route to manifesting your intention that made you re-consider some aspect of the bigger picture. Of course you'll be adding more and more information as you go about creating your intention, so what I'm talking about here are really course corrections – you feel you want your intention to have a different outcome than what you had originally intended, or you feel you need to clarify further some requirements on *how* your intention manifests. These are usually rare cases if you have taken time to feel the Bigger Picture of your intention, and assuming you are staying open to the forms and actions that present themselves as opportunities to explore.

DAY 24

Me: Feels like we're ready for tools to navigate the swampy, in-between time – from intention clarity to actual intention manifestation. I'm a little nervous or edgy about this phase – it feels like it's the most difficult, and where I'm most likely to get off track or give up.

II: Yes, the way you currently view this phase feels a bit like Atreyu trudging through the swamps of despair in the movie *The NeverEnding Story*. Even his brave horse got swallowed up in the mire, and Atreyu was only saved because of the protective amulet he wore around his neck.

Me: Yeah, so is one of the tools a protective amulet to avoid despair and discouragement while waiting for my intention to manifest?

II: No, it's time for you to adopt a different archetype for this phase of intention work so that you can be more playful and light-hearted, and not feel like you need to protect yourself from a dangerous universe. Albert Einstein got it when he said, "The most important decision we make is whether we believe we live in a friendly or hostile universe." The Universe Is A Friendly Place.

Me: OK. So, what's a new archetype I can use for this phase?

II: A long, enjoyable hike is a good analogy, because while you are looking forward to, and working toward, the end destination of the hike, you can also completely enjoy the experiences you are having along the way. In fact, isn't that the point of a long hike – to see and experience everything in the wilderness along the trail, or even off the beaten path? Otherwise you humans probably would have found a way to air-drop yourself in to the end destination or viewpoint.

Yes, this *is* a good analogy for you, because it will help you to value and appreciate the entire journey, not just the beginning intention and the end manifestation. Each intention really is an opportunity for you to experience new adventures that you would not have had access to if you hadn't set out toward the manifestation of it. So, lighten up and enjoy your hike!

Me: All right – that does feel a lot better already. So, what tools do you suggest for this hiking trip toward the manifested intention?

II: Well, obviously you'll bring your intention-compass with you in order to stay on track. Next, think in terms of nourishment. What will nourish you so that you have the energy to keep going, keep persisting toward manifesting your intention? Sometimes what nourishes you will be related to your intention – like sharing your intention with close friends, and feeling their enthusiasm and excitement added to yours as additional encouragement fuel. Sometimes your nourishment will be unrelated to your intention – like caring for your body, or taking a "mental-health" day. It's important that you incorporate your intention work into your overall, balanced, enjoyable lifestyle. Don't burn yourself out by putting too much forced attention on your intention, to the point that you are ignoring other aspects of your life.

Better, is to decide that *all* of your activities are working in harmony to move forward *all* of your intentions. With that belief, you will never have to feel like you need to sacrifice one part of your life in order for another to prosper.

Another thing you can do for nourishment is to explore perspectives about your intention. When you are hearing other people's ways of seeing the world, or even just broadening your own considerations of what's possible or how you can look at things, then you are allowing more Universal Energy to flood into you. And that flood of energy and connection to the *many* perspectives of the Universe is *very* nourishing – both to you (as a human viewpoint) and to your intention (as an idea that is seeking expression).

THE INTENTION IDEA

Me: Huh! So you're saying that additional perspectives and finding new ways of looking at something is nourishing?

II: Very nourishing! It's the stuff the Universe is made of – many perspectives and ways of experiencing. Adding more perspectives is one way the universe grows and unfolds. For the human experience, adding perspectives can get you out of a rut, or a repeating pattern loop, and get you moving forward again.

Me: Sounds extremely important!

II: Yes, putting one foot in front of the other – or adding one perspective after another – may be the most basic way for you to navigate this long hike of manifesting your intention. Even though it's simple, it's really the only thing that will get you there.

Me: Why do you equate adding perspectives with taking the next step on the hike, instead of physical action or effort being the thing that moves the intention forward?

II: Physical action and effort are in your supply kit for this phase of intention-work too, but you don't have to do a physical-world action in order to create a physical-world result, or to have forward movement on your path.

This concept may be more challenging for you to integrate since you are so used to physical-world, cause-and-effect stories of the world. In fact, many stories in your world about non-physical causes with physical-world results are often labeled as magical, miraculous, serendipitous, or even coincidence. All of these labels make it seem like it's not repeatable or sustainable. That's why we're working together – to help you see and explore the non-physical causes you can do (like exploring perspectives) to create repeatable, sustainable results.

THE INTENTION IDEA

Me: I can't help but feel a little suspicious that it will work. It feels like you're going to give me some magic spell to believe in, and if I believe just right, then I'll get results. And the deduction I have is, that if I don't get results, I must not have believed right or well enough.

II: Yes, these indoctrinations and beliefs about working with the unseen, energetic, non-physical realms have been pretty tangled up for humans for a while. And when you are very attached to operating with the physical-world rules, it can be more difficult to explore, practice, and grow your skills at working with the non-physical. For now, I suggest you keep an open mind, be OK with failures, and keep experimenting with the tools that feel best to you.

Me: So, consider another perspective and keep going?

II: Pretty much. We can revisit this topic again though. I know you have more questions about it, but let's keep unpacking our tools first.

Me: Sounds good!

DAY 25

II: So, on this long hike, you check your intention-compass as needed, you nourish yourself regularly so you can keep going, you keep considering and exploring other perspectives as a way of keeping moving forward energetically, and you take any actions in the physical world that feel aligned with your intention.

Me: How do I know if a physical action is aligned with my intention?

II: You usually have a sense of this when you consider the action – it feels overall good, or else you have a niggling sensation that something is wrong, off, or not-quite right. If you're not sure, wait for clarity. Do your best to get more information about the possible next step. And be OK with trying something and failing. Even if you have a mis-step, or even a giant fall, you're still on the adventurous path toward your manifested intention.

Which brings us to your emergency kit while hiking. In your experience of physical-world hiking, you often think of your emergency kit as something to have on hand, just in case, but it's rarely used. In our intention hike analogy, it would be better if you considered this kit to be supplies you draw on throughout your hike – it's expected that you will use them. Kind of like a novice hiker with new shoes – *of course* they will use the fresh pair of socks and moleskin in their emergency kit, in order to avoid getting bad blisters on their hike.

Me: OK, so it's kind of like additional supplies, since it's a long hike?

II: Yes, exactly. If your intention happens to manifest quickly, then you won't even think about these supplies. But with each intention you create, there's no guarantee how long your hike to manifestation will be, so it's better to be prepared to access and use these supplies *whenever* you need them.

Me: What's in this emergency supply kit?

II: These are your tools for increasing your persistence, amping up your faith, and for removing obstacles on your path.

Me: Oooh, those all sound like things I could use regularly!

II: Exactly! Let's start with tools for increasing your persistence, which in essence means how you apply and direct your will power.

Me: What's the difference between applying and directing will power?

II: Applying will power is like the amount of energy or power you put behind a punch. Directing will power is like knowing where to strike a board so it will break. If you don't apply your will power well, then you either won't have enough to get a result, or you'll have too much, so you create an explosion and a burnout from misuse of energy.

If you don't direct your will power well, it can feel like you're hitting your head against a brick wall with no result, or like you're totally off-target and unclear about what you're doing and why you're doing it.

Me: Makes sense. So how do I best apply and direct my will power?

II: First, you need a regular routine of exercising and strengthening your will power, so that your will muscle is well-developed and easy for you to use whenever you need it. Incidentally, if you're operating a belief that being "willful" is bad, you'll need to remove it in order to have full access to your will power. Or at least consider some additional perspectives on what it means to be willful.

THE INTENTION IDEA

You can strengthen your will by doing what you say you will do. That could be as simple as saying you're going to get up and walk to the kitchen, and then doing it. It can also be a more advanced use of will when you say and do something that you have some resistance to doing. Like, "I'm going to wash the pile of dishes on the kitchen counter."

Essentially, every time you say you're going to do something, *and* you do it, you are strengthening your will power – you are strengthening your muscle for using, applying, and directing your will. Every time you use your will to do something that you have some reluctance or resistance to doing, you are increasing your ability to direct your will and apply it to obstacles that you have created in your own mind.

Me: I feel like I need some help discerning when to use my will to push through on something I'm resisting doing, and when to consider it my intuition not to do that action.

II: Yes, in its effort to preserve the status quo, the human mind can get very tricky with this distinction. Here's something to consider the next time you are wondering whether to push through or back off and go a different route:

If you did push through, do you imagine feeling good about yourself for following through?

If yes, then it's not your intuition telling you to back off, it's the resistance in your current mind structure trying to keep things as they are. If no – if you imagine not feeling good about yourself for pushing through – then it's truly your intuition suggesting there is a better way. And, in either case, taking some time to explore other perspectives on the action-in-question will help you to either release the resistances in your mind, or find a different route that is more in alignment with your intuition.

Me: I'm starting to see how valuable the exploration of perspectives is for keeping moving forward, especially when I'm feeling blocked

THE INTENTION IDEA

or stuck.

II: Indeed.

Me: Let's say I've been practicing strengthening my will regularly. In the moments of intention work when I need more persistence, what do I need to do in order to apply and direct my will? And how do I know it's a moment when I need more persistence?

II: You know you need more persistence when what you've been doing so far has not yet manifested your intention. Just like you know you need to keep hiking because you haven't made it to the end goal of your hike yet. And just like on a hike, you will need to *honestly* check in with yourself to see if you first need nourishment, or a compass check, before pushing forward in the direction you're going. In fact, that's probably one of the best ways to confirm the *direction* of your will power – see if the action you're thinking of applying your will and energy toward is in alignment with your intention compass. If any part of the action feels off, or out-of-alignment, then explore perspectives on how it could be more aligned. Or, consider how you could course-correct with other actions, so that the whole collection of your actions *is* fully in alignment with your intention.

As for applying your will, if you are practicing using your will in your daily life actions, then it will be easier and easier to apply it to your intention work. It's like weight lifting – if you keep practicing with whatever weight you can lift now, then over time you will gradually be able to lift heavier and heavier weights. You might not be able to "move mountains" immediately, but regular practice, and gradually increasing the challenges you go after, enables you to "move mountains" in your future.

Me: What if I forget, or I don't want to practice? (I'm asking now because I know I can be prone to lapses in practice.) ☺

II: I never said you had to be perfect at this. If you lapse in your practice, forgive yourself and get back to your practice at whatever level you can do it now, in this moment. Even the decision to restart your practice is an act of will, so give yourself credit for creating a more advanced practice scenario: starting again after stopping takes a lot more will than continuing what is already in motion. See it as a challenge, and go for it. Don't spend time judging yourself over it. You wouldn't judge yourself about any outside-of-you challenge on this journey. And if you *would* judge yourself on how you use your will in any other scenario, consider exploring your perspectives and beliefs about that, so that you can loosen up those judgments and lighten up! ☺

DAY 26

Me: So, using my will regularly is how I increase my persistence. What's the tool for amping up my faith? And what do you mean by that, and when would I need to do it?

II: Just like *practicing* using your will helps you to be ready and able to apply it, as needed, to keep persisting in your intention work, you will also be *practicing* tools for amplifying your faith. Faith is essentially a belief in something you don't necessarily see or have evidence for, but you believe in it so strongly, with so much conviction, that it is real for you. Faith creates physical world experiences for you.

Faith, as a word, is often connected with religion or spirituality in most human minds. This is because, in religion and spirituality, you are working often with unseen concepts and energies that require a strong conviction and belief, in order to work with them. Outside of religion and spiritual doctrines, Faith is a tool you use to help bring into physical manifestation and physical experience something, anything, that you have decided is worth investing with your time, energy, and attention. It's like a shorthand way of saying, "I've decided to put a lot of focused energy and attention on making this ____ real for me, even when I have no physical evidence or signs that it is."

Me: Wow, when you put it like that, I can really see how faith is a strong component for manifesting an intention. But I'm also used to faith not manifesting into the physical world – it's just something you have, life-long, without necessarily ever seeing a physical result. Like faith in God and Heaven – you don't have physical proof of these (necessarily) until you die, and I'm not even sure if you find out for sure then. How is faith the same, or different, from this scenario I'm used to?

II: It's the same because Faith inherently is believing without *needing* proof, the promise of proof, or even a physical manifestation, in order to hold the belief. You are *choosing* to hold the belief with strong conviction that it is true, even if you *never* see a physical manifestation. You are deciding to structure your mind and your life around this belief, or set of beliefs, that you are holding with faith.

It's different, this use of faith in intention-work, because most often your intention *will* manifest into the physical world, and you will see the results of your faith realized into a physical form. But you don't know *when* it will manifest, or how. It might be in the next hour, the next year, later in your lifetime, or even beyond your lifetime – like the intention to build a cathedral, or plant a forest, that only your children's children will get to see. Some intentions are so monumentally big in scope, direction, and intended effects that they do take lifetimes to realize, so they require a lot of faith from everyone who is holding that intention along the way, in order to keep it going and manifest it.

Me: It feels like that intention wave analogy again.

II: Yes, exactly. A very large and long wave needs a lot of continual energy supplied to it, and within it, in order to traverse a very wide ocean, and to eventually manifest on the shore.

Me: How is energy supplied to it versus within it?

II: In the context of intentions, the initial passion, excitement, and clear directions of the intention get it started. As it progresses, the environment may supply more energy to it – like if it is aligned well with other Flows in the Universe, and those complementary energies are added to the intention wave you started.

Energy is supplied within an intention-wave when you allow all that passion, excitement, and clear direction to recycle and build on itself. Like revisiting your intention compass to remind yourself why it's important to you, and getting excited all over again. Or like seeing something in your environment that reminds you of your intention, and feeling that warm glow of excitement, and *knowing* you are going in the right direction and focusing on the right intention for you.

Me: OK, cool! So how do I keep amping up my faith in order to keep my intention wave going no matter what?

II: Practice, practice, practice and Attention, attention, attention. To amplify your faith means you keep putting your attention on your intention *with* an attitude that it will succeed no matter what. You may also need to let go some of your attachments to time and insistences on *when* your intention will manifest. To do this, you might try visualizing what it would be like if your intention manifested at timespans that are further and further out. Like in one month, in one year, in ten years, late in your lifetime, and in another lifetime (either yours if you believe in reincarnation and want to try that perspective, or in your lineage's lifetimes if you want to consider your intention as a gift to the world that manifests after your lifespan).

If you meet resistance in your mind-space to visualizing your intention manifesting later, then you may want to revisit how your intention fits with the Bigger Picture of the Universe. You may also need to look at the actions you are taking in order to manifest your intention. If you don't like who you are becoming on route to your manifested intention, then you need to adjust your tactics to be more in alignment with your sense of integrity and the Flow of the Universe.

DAY 27

Me: I can feel how often I get so focused on the carrot – the juicy end goal of my intention – that I have no attention on, or even available for, what's happening right now. It's almost like I'm resisting this in-between time and yearning for the "arrival state" of having realized my goal.

II: Yes, this is a common problem resulting from minds that are trained at young ages to get to the result, get the right answer, get to the point, cross the finish line, move up a level, and finish what you've started. You have a lot of indoctrinations that focus much more on finishing and completing than on enjoying, experiencing, savoring, being, and exploring. Interestingly, the rest of the Universe – outside of your mind – is much more attuned to the energies of exploration, expansion, and experience. The Greater Universe does *not* have a goal to complete or finish all this life-stuff. ☺

Me: Good point. I hadn't really looked at it that way. And when I look at my intentions I want to create, I still see them more like goals to achieve than as an adventurous journey to go on and explore. Except for this one with you – you've helped me a lot to simply enjoy our conversations and explorations together. Even though I feel there will be some major milestone completion points in our work together, I'm also just thrilled to be enjoying our explorations. It feels more like an ongoing relationship we are building than a task or project to get done.

II: Yes, this is exactly the feel of working on an intention that will help you hold the broader, more expansive, and widened-back view of your intentions. This keeps you out of time-pressures to complete things, and keeps you more in tune with your Faith that all will unfold with perfect timing.

THE INTENTION IDEA

Me: What if my intention is for something that is time-based? How do I amp up my Faith in my intention manifesting when I really do need it by a certain deadline? Like, what if I have an intention to earn enough money to pay my rent at the end of the month?

II: With time-sensitive intentions like this, Faith is only one of several tools you will need to use in your intention-work. In this example, the way you apply your Faith is by increasing your conviction that everything is all right, things always work out for you, and that you will intuit what your next steps are – and take them. Holding these convictions, and acting on them, empowers you to work with all components of the Universe to manifest your intention.

And then, you are also using your Will to keep persevering on your path. Keep taking the next steps that are laid out in front of you – whether they are physical world actions, or they are mental space actions like removing obstacles and limitations in your consciousness.

And that brings us to the third component of your "emergency supply kit": tools for removing obstacles.

Me: I definitely need those. Sometimes I feel like I have rocks in my head.

II: You do. And most people do. Really, if you think of the obstacles you encounter like they are rocks in your head, you might be able to see how, at one point, they were valuable to you. Maybe you used those rocks as stepping stones to get toward something else, or as barriers to hide behind and protect you when you felt threatened in some way. The point is, they aren't put there randomly. At the time, it seemed like a good idea. But for where you are now, and where you want to get to, they are pretty much obstacles on your currently intended path.

Me: So how do I move them around, or bust them up, or otherwise get past them?

II: First, it helps to know what you're dealing with. If you are feeling blocked or limited in *any* way, it's a good time to do some inner exploration. You could do this inner exploration with meditation, writing, drawing, or a simple contemplation of different perspectives on the area where you feel blocked. The point of any technique you use is to honestly and compassionately take a look at where and how you feel blocked. What's really going on here? Why is it important? What are the feelings and sensations involved? What are the thoughts, ideas, and beliefs, especially the ones on repeating loops, around this topic?

Once you can look at the many aspects of the block from a place of observation (rather than from feeling stuck in the middle of it), then you have more Awareness-level control over the rock. With that Awareness-level control you will be more able to move the rock, bend it, bust it up, or otherwise get around it (since now you know where its edges are – where it is, and where it isn't, in your mind and your life).

Me: Is seeing the entirety of the rock really enough to get past it?

II: That depends on the rock. Some are more rooted in place than others, and some are actually part of a whole rock pile. Just know that full awareness of the rock is your first step, and for some rocks (limitations/obstacles) that will be enough for you to be able to maneuver around them, or toss them out of your mind, because they no longer have value for you.

Me: What do I do if it's a stuck rock, or part of a rock pile?

II: First of all, draw on your persistence practice. Be OK that it isn't moving quickly, and keep using your will to explore its many aspects as you look for its value and how you might move beyond it now. Just like hiking in the wilderness, there may be times that you take a long time to get around an obstacle on your path. See this as part of your journey and you will be able to hold a more positive and effective attitude toward your current experience. You might not be ready to embrace being a professional rock buster, when you'd rather be hiking an open meadow, but you can still choose to appreciate the strength building and inner exploration that you are getting on this part of your journey.

Me: OK, I can feel a practice, practice, practice mantra coming on...

II: To some extent, yes. You know how life patterns and lessons can often appear like onion layers, or like the spiral of a shell ... you can handle an outer layer of the onion, or shell, and go along life feeling much better, only to discover another layer that resembles the previous one you have handled. It's important that you recognize that this new layer is not the same as the first. You are not going backwards, but in fact you are evolving to greater and greater understanding of the core issue and additional aspects of it that you were not able to see or handle with the first layer. In other words, it's OK if a topic seems to be repeating. The goal is not to be done and finished with *all* issues / obstacles / limitations. The goal is to handle whatever obstacle / issue / limitation is in front of you on your path now, and keep moving. So yes, practice, practice, practice. Or maybe a better mantra for you is "keep moving forward."

DAY 28

Me: It seems like handling these rocks (limitations) will require more tools than the questions you offered to help me see all the aspects of the "rock." I've recently looked for, and found, lots of different tools for removing obstacles and resistances. Even just now, as I used your "Rock Questions" to better understand an issue that's been repeating for me, at the end of answering the questions I could see it clearly enough to use one of my Avatar tools to remove the beliefs that were at the root of the obstacle. Is there anything else you want to offer to help people remove limitations?

II: No. There are so many varieties of tools already created into the world that help people remove obstacles once they are found. I find it's better to let people continue to seek, attract, and find the tools that resonate the most for them at this time. In the context of our intention-work together, the best tool for you to remember to use on obstacles is the set of questions I gave you. These questions help you to see the rock from many perspectives, and truly be *aware* of the rock from outside of the "stuckness" of it. You'd be surprised how often that level of awareness is enough for you to be able to keep moving forward on your path toward your realized intention. And if for any reason it isn't enough, then your persistence, Faith, and intention compass will help you to navigate to the perfect set of tools for handling that specific obstacle. Trust yourself, and your intuition, that you will always be guided to the perfect solutions and experiences for the unfoldment of *your* life path … and you will be. ☺

Me: OK, that feels good. I feel well supplied for taking a long (or short) hike toward the manifestation of my intention. I guess the only last piece I'm not entirely sure about, in this phase, is what to do if I get really off track? Like what if I lose interest in my intention, or get sidetracked into doing something else instead? How do I handle that scenario?

II: It's OK if this happens. Life is full of interesting things to explore, and no exploration or experience is value-less. Some experiences *you* might find more valuable than others, based on your current point of view. But from a Universal, Big Picture perspective, *every* experience is adding to the unfoldment and evolution of the whole Universe.

So, let's say you get "off-track." And let's say you come to realize you're off-track from what you originally set out to do. Now you get to decide if you still want to manifest the intention you had started to create, or if you want to deliberately let it go and choose to create a different intention instead. It's that simple: decide to continue on your original path, or abort that project, let it go, and go after something else instead.

Me: I feel like there's something inherently wrong with deciding to abort an intention – like once you've started something you should finish it.

II: That idea is the result of indoctrination. The Universe is in no way attached to intentions manifesting. And in fact, if the intention is really something that is "right-timed" to Flow into physical manifestation, then it will come through some other channel that is more aligned with the energy of it. It's totally OK if your energy shifts, changes, and aligns differently than how you started out. Really, you're supposed to grow, adapt, and evolve in different directions based on the experiences you are having. So, stay flexible and open in your outlook, and always tune in to what feels most in alignment with *your* Heart Path. It's true what is often said, that you really can't go wrong when you Follow Your Heart. (Though sometimes you need to improve your abilities to listen to what your Heart is truly saying.)

Me: How do I do that?

II: That's a bigger topic worth discussing another time. For now, keep focusing on your intention-work and using all these tools, and you will find your skills at listening to your Heart are improving quite naturally.

DAY 29

Me: When you first talked about this in-between phase of intention manifestation, you also mentioned tools for feeling for next steps. What do I need to be aware of in that context?

II: Your work and exploration of trying on different perspectives helps immensely with this. When you keep looking for another viewpoint, and *another* viewpoint, and *another* viewpoint, then you are less likely to lock yourself into your own perceptions of how you think your intention should manifest.

Exploring perspectives and viewpoints about your intention, and about the possibilities you see as the potential next step, helps you to identify even more possible next steps. It also helps you more accurately feel which next step is most appropriate for you now. Only when you are open to all possibilities, can you truly trust your intuition for which possibility to act on. Otherwise you are very likely to be acting from a biased opinion of how you think the Universe should work. Yes, that's as silly as it sounds: you thinking the Universe should work a certain way. While you can tap in to the Universal Flow and influence it, only when you get out of your made-up-mind can you really *feel* the Universally best next step.

Me: Anything else, in addition to exploring viewpoints, that will help me feel the next step?

II: If it's not clear to you what to do next, then there are a couple of things you can revisit:

1. Look at your intention-compass again, and take some time to really feel your connection with your intention. If you like visualization, this would be a good time to visualize and feel your intention fully manifested. Explore with your imagination what your intention might be like, using *all* your senses. While in a relaxed state, enjoy

spending time with the Vision of your intention. Do not put pressure on your intention to "show you the way" to manifest it. Just hang out together.

2. Look for any resistances, reactions, or sense of limitation you feel in your mind-space, in your heart-space, or even in your environment and people around you. If there's any area of your life that doesn't feel like it has *some* kind of forward momentum flow in it, then use your tools for removing obstacles to loosen up this log jam and get the energy moving again. Every part of your life is connected, so a log jam, or limiting belief, in one area of your life can easily be slowing down your forward momentum in other areas of your life. That's not to say that every area of your life has to be perfect in order for you to create your intention. But it is to say, that creating forward momentum of *any* amount, in every area of your life, helps *all* of your intentions to move forward.

So, fully explore how you're doing in all aspects of your life, and with *all* your intentions. Freeing up obstacles, limiting beliefs, and other limitations in one area will automatically feed more energy, power, and clarity of direction to your intention, and to *every* area of your life. You are a Holistic system evolving, and no exploration or evolution happens without impact on your whole System of Beingness.

Me: Mmmm. I like the feel of that!

DAY 30

Me: Let's talk about this "birthing phase" of fully manifesting my intention into reality. You said I'd need tools for keeping out of egotistical pride, and for staying connected to the Bigger Picture. Why is that important in this phase?

II: As your intention materializes into the physical realm, it's natural for you to feel increased excitement and joy. It's like, as your intention becomes real, your feelings about your intention amplify as well. Plus, you have a lot of societal indoctrinations that have conditioned you to have ecstatic responses when you are getting something you have been wanting. So, it's normal for you to feel like you're "flying high" when your intention manifests.

It's plenty fine for you to enjoy this natural, high-vibration of emotions. But, if you don't also use tools to keep yourself grounded and connected to people around you, and to what's really happening in the moment, then you can start to spin out of control, and even lose the connection and momentum with your intention. Your connection and momentum are important to be aware of, because the manifestation of an intention is never "the end of the line," or a final completion, or a stopping point. The Universe is *always* evolving, and every manifested intention is moving that evolution forward. So, feeling and connecting to your intention from this greater context of evolution will help you to better ride your wave to shore, as well as connect your manifested intention with your next intentions to manifest.

Me: Sounds good, but how do I do that? It feels like a very big Universal perspective to hold when, instead, I'm usually so super excited for my own human experience in the moment.

II: Yes, it's a stretch for you to step out of that mind-creation that I'll call the "glory of winning." But, it's a worthwhile stretch, because

THE INTENTION IDEA

the experience of feeling so deeply and broadly connected with everyone and everything in the Universe is so much, well, *More*. Beyond words really, so make sure you use the tools and allow yourself to really experience what we're talking about in order to have a visceral, real-life understanding. Using the tools will help remind you to connect with this Bigger Picture perspective and experience, instead of following the mind's cravings for the smaller prize of "winner-glory."

Me: OK, so what are the tools?

II: First, to help you get outside of a mind that is overrun with Egotistical Pride, you will want to see how your current experience is valuable to every other person on the planet. You are using your perspective-shifting abilities to get out of the "me, myself, and mine" viewpoints. And, you are carrying your accomplishment outward as a service and gift to the world. When you are focused on bringing your intention into the physical realms as a benefit to others, as a gift to the whole world, then you are less likely to focus your attention on yourself and on what you're getting from it.

Me: This feels like it may be hard to do sometimes. I can see how often I want something for my own experience of it, not because I've decided it could be helpful to others.

II: It's OK that this is a stretch, and not an automatic perspective for you. And it's OK that you want things for your own experience. Remember that you are an expression of the Universe, so creating for your own experience (as it may seem) is also creating for the experience of the Universe. It just depends on how you look at it – *and* how attached you are to having it all to yourself vs. sharing the experience freely with the Universe.

Me: How do I share an experience freely with the Universe?

II: You stay open and connected to the Universe. Let others see and feel the experience you are having. Avoid hierarchical thinking about your manifested intention accomplishment, and instead hold the belief and attitude that others can create what they want to create as easily and grace-fully as you just have – and even better.

In fact, you can see yourself as a Pioneer every time you manifest an intention, because each time you do, you are carving a path in consciousness for *a* way to bring an intention into reality. Even if no one ever manifests an intention the way you just did (and most every manifestation will be slightly or massively different), you are always re-emphasizing to others that we all have the Power to create what we prefer. We all have the power to take an ethereal intention-idea and turn it into a physical reality. Choose to view all manifested intentions with the same kind of respect a wilderness explorer would have for a fellow explorer who has passed through the unknowns of uncharted territory, and emerged with a map of where they've been and a big smile on their face for the adventure they have completed. Truly, we are all in this together, exploring, experiencing, and sharing our experiences through our willingness to be connected with one another.

From this attitude of connection and continued exploration, it's very difficult to also hold the egotistical pride idea of "mine." Let that idea go, and enjoy the connection of your intention-wave with all the many other intention-waves in our great, big intention-sea.

DAY 31

Me: I feel so empowered and uplifted by what you've said about focusing on connection and gifting my intentions to the world. It's hard to imagine I'd need anything else to stay out of egotistical pride, but I also know that ego-mind can be a tricky and sticky mindset to get out of. What other tools do you suggest for managing that ego-mind, especially once I'm in it?

II: Yes, what I've told you so far about shifting your perspective to the Universal, connected, and gifting viewpoints is very helpful, and revisiting that part of our conversation is always a good first step. Another quick thing you can do to step out of the ego-mind, is to practice kindness toward others. Deliberately do kind acts for all the people around you, and for people you think of, in any and every moment. When you are deliberately kind, you are starting to get out of a selfish "me and mine" mindset, and you are extending your attention outwards toward others with an intention to be helpful. This practice of kindness will get your feet moving in the direction of being helpful to others, connecting with people to better understand what they need, and feeling the value of helping *everyone* succeed, not just yourself. Really, "you" only win when everyone wins.

Me: Feels like a mindset practice – always looking for how my actions are helping others, rather than always looking out for myself and only taking care of my own needs and wants.

II: Yes, exactly. The more you practice creating win-win situations – where everyone feels cared for, satisfied, and heard – then the more easily you can hold the Universal perspective. Also, when you are creating win-win situations, you are less likely to be caught in an ego-mind trap that really doesn't go very far. Egotistical pride successes have a limited shelf-life – the high from them wears off quickly, and you are soon looking for the next accomplishment to achieve. In contrast, Universal win-win successes always have a forward momentum that builds toward the next co-creation of awesome experiences that everyone can enjoy. The possibilities from this way of creating are limitless and abundantly flowing.

Me: So, Big Picture / Universal perspective and acts of kindness. Anything else?

II: There are many practices already designed to help you get out of the ego-mind and open more to your Universal / Higher Self / Heart-Space connections. You can use meditations, world peace visualizations, and even some body and energy system techniques that help you get out of the logical mind frames and more into a Quantum Heart-View. The last tool I'll suggest here, since it is near and dear to your heart, is the Avatar compassion exercise. When you use this exercise, you are automatically moving from your head to your heart, and experiencing more of your connection and oneness with others – who you might have been holding at arm's length (or farther). Tools like this help you to feel, experience, and embody the idea that "we're all in this together." These tools are immensely helpful for getting you out of the ego-mind and back into your natural connection with all that is.

Keep practicing! 🖖

The Avatar Compassion Exercise[4]

> Increase the amount of compassion in the world.
> ## Compassion Exercise
>
> **Instructions:** This exercise can be done anywhere that people congregate (airports, malls, parks, beaches, etc.). It should be done on strangers, unobtrusively, from some distance. Try to do all five steps on the same person. Expected results are a personal sense of peace.
>
> **STEP 1** With attention on the person, repeat to yourself:
> **Just like me, this person is seeking some happiness for his/her life.**
>
> **STEP 2** With attention on the person, repeat to yourself:
> **Just like me, this person is trying to avoid suffering in his/her life.**
>
> **STEP 3** With attention on the person, repeat to yourself:
> **Just like me, this person has known sadness, loneliness and despair.**
>
> **STEP 4** With attention on the person, repeat to yourself:
> **Just like me, this person is seeking to fulfill his/her needs.**
>
> **STEP 5** With attention on the person, repeat to yourself:
> **Just like me, this person is learning about life.**
>
> ### Variations:
> 1. May be done by couples and family members to increase understanding of each other.
> 2. May be done on old enemies and antagonists still present in your memories.
> 3. May be done on other life forms.
>
> This is one of thirty exercises that can be found in
> *ReSurfacing®: Techniques for Exploring Consciousness* by Harry Palmer.
> *Excerpted with permission.* ©1994, 2015

---

[4] Excerpted with permission by Harry Palmer / Star's Edge, Inc. The Avatar Compassion Project was started in October, 2009 to increase the amount of compassion in the world. Over 6 million compassion cards have already been given to strangers all around the world, including many world leaders. You can learn more about the Compassion Project, order compassion cards, and donate to the project of giving compassion cards to world leaders here: http://theavatarcourse.com/the-compassion-project-eng.html

DAY 32

Me: It seems like the same tools that you've mentioned for keeping out of egotistical pride will also help me to stay connected to the Bigger Picture. But I'm wondering now, if you also recommend tools specific to enhancing my connection to the Bigger Picture?

II: Yes, they are one and the same. But if you want to focus even more on your connection to the Bigger Picture, then you can focus your meditations, visualizations, contemplations, and interactions on the Universal perspectives of your intention in the greater, whole sea of intentions. This includes exploring how your manifesting intention benefits people you know, people you don't know, communities, societies, humanity, the planet (all living experiences on it), and the Universe (as an ever expanding and evolving system that tends toward harmony and adventure). Most humans are used to creating what they want because they want it. When you deliberately focus your attention on any aspect of this Bigger Picture of "benefitting others," you will be connecting and aligning your intention with a greater Flow of Power than you could muster on your own. This is not Power you can take, steal, or leverage for your own devices – it is Power freely available and immediately applied to intentions that are in alignment with the current direction of Universal Evolution.

Me: How do I find out what the current direction is, and if my intention is in alignment with it?

II: A simple, quick test is what Buckminster Fuller asked himself of all his inventions: "Does this support life?" A more detailed understanding could be had by asking, "How does this intention benefit others, and does everyone win?"

Like everything we've been exploring together, the more you practice all these tools for working with intentions, the more you will be able to sense, feel, experience, and harmonize with the current Flow of the Universe. The more you get out of your mind's attachments to how it thinks things should be, and get connected with your heart and Higher Self's understandings and appreciation of "what-is," the easier your experience of *all* of this intention journey.

DAY 33

Me: OK, feels like we're ready for what you called the final phase: integrating, experiencing, enjoying, and expanding from the physical manifestation. Whatcha got to say about this phase of intention-work?

II: This is, perhaps, an often-overlooked aspect of intention-work. It's also one of my favorite phases, because this is when you become the most fully aware of how your intention interacts and integrates with all the other intentions in the great, big intention sea. *And,* you get to co-create an awesome evolution of next steps from all the individually manifesting intentions. It's really operating on the leading edge of evolution, at the cusp of the ethereal and physical realms combined.

One of the things you'll get to do during this phase is fully enjoy, savor, relish, delight in, and full-body experience the physical form of your intention. You have been working with the intention mostly in the etheric realms while *you* are in a physical body. Now, instead of taking a virtual tour of your "castle in the sky," you'll get to actually go inside the castle, touch the walls, sit on the seats, and explore and experience it for real. It's the most delicious thing ever, to get to experience in physical form what you have been interacting with in mental, emotional, and other-realm spaces. So be sure to make time to enjoy it, savor it, and treat these moments of manifestation with the utmost respect and appreciation. It is truly a sacred moment to birth an intention into reality.

Me: Wow. I can feel how it can really be as sacred as giving birth – it really is bringing something new into the world, that wasn't here before, and giving it life.

II: Yes, it is that sacred. And so, your primary tools for this phase are to treat the moments of manifesting your intention sacredly.

That means slowing down your mind, being present, reverent, and respectful of what is happening now, and feeling and expressing your appreciation. How you do these things may look different with each intention, but as long as you have the feel of sacred respect while you enjoy exploring and appreciating your manifested intention, you'll be all right with whatever form that expression takes.

Me: This makes me think of award ceremonies where the award winner is thanking everyone who supported them in their work, or an author's acknowledgments page.

II: Yes, those are some forms of respect and appreciation that may be appropriate. Thanking people, and feeling and expressing gratitude for how your intention has manifested, increases your connection with the present moment, and your connection with *all* of the elements of the Universe that have contributed to the creation – both seen and unseen.

Me: Do you have any suggestions for how to handle my mind when I'm feeling unworthy of the manifested creation? Like if my intention manifests really quickly and easily, I often feel like I don't deserve to have it this good, or this easy.

II: Yes, this is an important mind-trick to be aware of, and to address. Your human and societal indoctrinations include a lot of beliefs about the value of hard work, earning your rewards, and pulling yourself up by the bootstraps. If you over-identify with these concepts of hard work, it limits your ability to take in and receive some of the more Grace-filled, easy, smooth, and lightning-quick manifestations. The Universe can create into Physical Form at any speed. But what you, as a co-creator, feel comfortable allowing into your experience, will determine the rate at which you actually manifest.

Me: That's so weird. I'm used to thinking of the speed of my manifestation as being dependent on my environment, not on my beliefs or comfort level. Like if something hasn't manifested yet, it must be because some elements in my environment need to be put in place first, or some physical obstacles need to be overcome.

II: Yes, you in physical form quickly get attached to physical form ways of perceiving creation. You know, hammer this nail into that board, and slowly build a fence. While you are in a physical playground, you *will* have creations that require physical actions and effort in order to manifest. But you are also, at the same time, in an etheric-realm playground. You always have access to the etheric-realm tools for creating, that are typically much faster than the physical-realm tools.

Me: That's fascinating that I'm in two different playgrounds at the same time! How does that work?

II: How it works isn't important to our discussion. *That* it works is how and why you are able to work with intentions and bring them into physical reality. The more you allow and accept that you are operating (always) in the physical *and* etheric realms, the easier it will be for you to accept and receive the lightning-fast and easy manifestations that can sometimes happen from working more and more with the etheric realms.

Me: This is something I've been meaning to ask you about. From a physical-realm perspective, working with the unseen, etheric realms often feels like magic. I have no good explanation for how I created this thing into existence, and no idea how to repeat my success. I also feel like it's a bit taboo to talk about or practice. I fear that working with the unseen makes me impractical, illogical, or ungrounded. What are your perspectives and suggestions about this aspect of intention-work?

II: Well, your society has been changing a lot, and more and more people are becoming aware of, sensitive to, and engaging with the unseen realms of existence. If you think about it, it wasn't that long ago that human's science ventures into the unseen, non-physical realms were mostly crude psychology and theoretical philosophies. Religion and spiritual practices probably had the most focus on working with unseen realms, but that was (and is) accompanied by a lot of beliefs and indoctrinations.

So, really, it's OK that it feels a bit new and vulnerable for you to more and more openly, directly, and deliberately explore how to work with unseen realms. You are sorting through quite a few established beliefs about what it means to work outside of the physical realms. You are also "growing new wings," or developing new skills and senses, for working in a realm that is much more subtle, and not always as obvious when you are operating as a physical body. Be easy with yourself and trust the process of your evolution. Just like the first people to use mobile phones were admired, *and* laughed at, for their venture into uncharted territories, you as a pioneer may be seen as weird, strange, abnormal, and doing things that don't make sense to people invested in the status quo. Just like with mobile phones, your etheric realm skills may someday become a ubiquitous technology or tool that most people have, and it would be surprising if you didn't use it. For now, see yourself as a Pioneer on the cutting edge of new human technology, and enjoy the evolution and development of these tools into a lifestyle that serves you, all of humanity, and the planet for the better.

DAY 34

Me: So, you've told me about savoring my created intention. What about tools for expanding from what is created toward what intentions to create next?

II: As long as you are staying in an attitude of gratitude, and fully connecting with and appreciating everyone and every idea that is stirred up, uncovered, or coming forward as a result of your created intention, then the next steps in the evolution and expansion from your intention will reveal themselves with perfect timing.

Perhaps the best advice I can give you for this phase is to stay open, keep enjoying and appreciating what-is, and stay *observant* of the responses and possibilities. There is no immediate need for action (typically), but you do need to maintain your physical / emotional / mental state of curiosity, adventure, and appreciation. Very often, the creation of an intention will reveal new teammates and partners for you to co-create with on a next intention. Follow the genuine appreciation and joyful enthusiasm to feel for what's next.

And sometimes there isn't an obvious next step that evolves from an intention. From a human perspective, it probably feels like some intentions are created, and then just fizzle and die. But just because there is no longer a lot of attention directed toward that creation, does not mean it was not, or is not, still valuable now.

Some intentions are appropriately acting as stepping stones that get you to a new vantage point from which you can see the next possible creations. Some intentions are created in order for you and others to practice and learn a skill set, but that skill set is applied to a totally different direction of intentions. And some intentions are created for the joy of the creator in the moment of creating, and when they are done, they are dissolved back into a sea of possibilities. Your role as a human is *not* to make a treasure trove of ever-lasting, physical-world creations. Your role is to evolve and expand from the experiences of *every* creation. This includes the intentions that have been started and stopped before manifesting, and the intentions that were manifested and seemingly left behind, because they are no longer incorporated into your current focus of attention.

Me: So, no tools – just appreciation and openness to exploration?

II: Those ways of perceiving the world *are* tools. If you really feel a need to ritualize it, or mark the next steps of your manifested intention, you could celebrate its birthday, or give it an achievement award for making it all the way into the physical realm. Whatever you choose to do, do it lightly, with appreciation and gratitude, and without attachment or seriousness. Don't try to "lock in" your intention into any particular form – even once it has manifested into a form. Intentions and their manifested physical forms are meant to be malleable so that the Universe can recycle and reuse any necessary elements for the *next* intentions at the leading edge of our evolution. To everything there is a season … enjoy it and move on. ☺

DAY 35

Me: Now that you've described all the tools for all the phases of intention-work, I really want to sum it up into a short, bulleted list for easy reference. Is that OK?

II: Yes, that's OK. I recognize that the human mind often craves and works well with structure, clear organization, sorting, and defining things. The important part of our co-creation is that you don't turn our conversations and explorations together into rules, or "shoulds," or "have tos." I have deliberately left a lot of room for creativity in interpretation, application, and further exploration for *all* the tools we have discussed. There is no one, right way to create an intention. So it's important, in each moment, to stay open and flexible to the possibilities of what next step and approach is best for you.

Intention-Work Easy Reference Guide
II: Remember to Lighten Up! ☺

The Beginning
Coming up with an intention

Focus:
- Quiet the mind
- Tune in to the flow of the universe
- Listen and feel for what's needed
- Imagine/intuit/explore new possibilities

Tools:
- Meditations
- Creative Arts
- Spend Time Observing
- Playing with Words

(Reading starts on Day 22)

THE INTENTION IDEA

Direction
Getting a full sense of your intention

Focus:
- Explore intention more deeply
- Feel into what its manifestation would be like

Tools:
- Intention Statements
- Vision Boards
- Mind Maps

(Reading starts on Day 23)

The Hike
In-Between the chosen intention and its manifestation

Focus:
- Experience new adventures along the way
- Align actions with the intention direction
- Persistence, Faith, and Removing Obstacles

Tools:
- Check Intention Compass and Feel for Next Steps
- Nourishment of body, mind, and intention
- Adding and Exploring Perspectives
- Physical Action and Effort

THE INTENTION IDEA

Emergency Supply Kit (for longer hikes):
- Increase Persistence: Practice Applying and Directing Will Power
- Amplify Your Faith: Put Attention on your Intention with an Attitude that it will succeed
    - Visualize what it would be like if your intention manifested at timespans that are further and further out
    - Review how your intention fits with the Bigger Picture of the Universe
    - Increase your conviction that everything is all right and that you will intuit what your next steps are – and take them
- Remove Obstacles: Use the "Rock Questions" for an inner exploration of the area where you feel blocked:
    - What's really going on here?
    - Why is it important?
    - What are the feelings and sensations involved?
    - What are the thoughts, ideas, and beliefs, especially the ones on repeating loops, around this topic?

(Reading starts on Day 24)

Physical Manifestation
Birthing the intention into reality

Focus:
- Keep out of egotistical pride
- Stay connected to the Bigger Picture

Tools:
- See how your current experience is valuable to every other person on the planet
- Practice Kindness toward everyone
- Do The Avatar Compassion Exercise

THE INTENTION IDEA

- Create win-win situations where everyone feels cared for, satisfied, and heard
- Ask: "Does this support life?" or "How does this intention benefit others, and does everyone win?"

(Reading starts on Day 30)

Experience & Evolution
Integrating & expanding into new intention waves

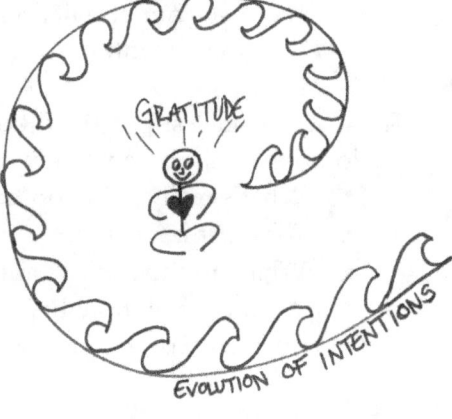

Focus:
- Become aware of how your intention interacts with all intentions
- Co-create an evolution of next steps
- Slow down your mind, be present, reverent, and respectful of what is happening now
- Feel and express your appreciation

Tools:
- Express Gratitude
- Acknowledge that you are operating (always) in the physical *and* etheric realms
- Stay open and *observant* of the responses and possibilities
- Appreciate and be Open to Exploration

(Reading starts on Day 33)

DAY 36

Me: So, we've got this fun, easy reference list now, for all the phases of manifestation and related tools. After reading through everything again, and looking at the easy reference guide, I feel a little overwhelmed. That's a lot of tools to remember to use. I'm afraid I won't be good at applying all of them, at their relevant timings, during an intention's manifestation.

II: Rest easy with that thought. The whole point of sharing these perspectives and tools for intention-work, is to connect you more with your innate abilities to work in both the physical and etheric realms and manifest intentions. Your mind can get carried away sometimes when it wants to apply order and structure to a very creative and intuitive process. This is a good example of how the "right and wrong" game can trip you up. As soon as you decide that there's a "right" way to do things, you have now also created many "wrong" ways, that don't match up with the ideal, "right" way you created in your mind.

The whole point of these tools, and our conversations, is to help you connect more, and stay connected, with the Universal Flow. In the Flow, there is no right or wrong. There is alignment with the greater flow, and there are many other ways of looking at things that are all worthy of consideration. If you lock yourself into seeing things a certain way, you reduce, or even remove, the possibilities of Flows in your life that may actually be beneficial to you. The advice to stay open and observant, and to *lighten up*, is probably the most important focus for you, across all phases of intention-work.

From this light, open, and observant Place of Beingness, you are not prone to overwhelm, "right and wrong" games, or any other confusions the mind's indoctrinations may have in store. Just keep returning to this place, this still-point, this *YOU* that is light, open, and observant. From here you can see, feel, hear, know, and explore what is a good next step for you now.

Me: Thanks, I needed that.

I do still have a question about how to integrate, incorporate, and apply these tools. I feel like there are a lot of people introducing tools, exercises, or "their way of doing things" into the world, as if their particular tools are the missing piece someone needs in order to finally, Truly be successful. What's your perspective on this phenomenon? And are these tools you've offered any different?

II: It's OK that there are many tools and perspectives being offered into the world. Ideally, everyone would see the Bigger Picture of each offering as "another way of looking at things to consider." While it would be nice if the providers, and the recipients, did not get attached to the tools as if they are the one-and-only right way, or rules for success, or a panacea – it's also OK. It's OK that many humans are still very much attracted to these right-and-wrong kinds of mental structures and rules for successful living. You will all eventually evolve beyond those structures to a more fluid, open, and appreciative approach to all life experiences. You will evolve faster when you don't make "right-and-wrong approaches" wrong. ☺

You may have noticed that some of the tools we've discussed draw on pre-existing tools. What makes our conversation about intention-work different is exactly this open, fluid, and appreciative approach. Focusing more on the Bigger Picture, and the Intention and Direction of each tool, is much more important than which tool you use, or when and how you use it.

Me: That feels like my qigong classes, when my teacher reminds us to focus more on our intention for accessing high-level energies than the specific mechanics of how we are moving our bodies around in the different formations.

II: Yes, exactly. Intention and attitude can carry you, even if or when your physical-world tools and actions aren't "perfect" (according to someone's opinion of what "perfect" is).

Me: How do I best integrate, incorporate, and apply all these tools you've given me?

II: Follow your heart. If one or more tools calls to you right now, then explore with it, play with it, try it out on an intention you are working with. You can use the Easy Reference Guide to find an intention phase to focus on, or to spark your interest in a specific tool. Read through the guide to see if anything resonates for you right now. Or, you could also turn to a page of our conversations and read what we've been talking about. When you are holding your intention lightly in your field of attention – with appreciation and care – it's quite natural for there to be a flow of synchronous ideas, resources, and sparks for what to explore next. Stay open, observant, and appreciative. (Like I said, it's good advice).

PART 3

FOLLOW YOUR HEART

DAY 37

Me: What's next? I feel like we've covered a lot of ground, from all my questions about intentions, to our conversations about the intention-work phases, to the easy reference guide of tools for manifesting intentions. Where do we go from here?

II: Oh, the places you'll go! (I couldn't resist referencing the light and fun spirit of Dr. Seuss.) And really, the adventurous attitude that Dr. Seuss presented in his books is always a good place to start. Feel for what you'd like to explore and experience next, where you are most curious, and what topics and questions attract your attention.

Me: I'd definitely like to talk with you more about following my heart. I feel like you've referenced that as a bigger topic several times. Maybe now we can go down that rabbit hole, and explore more deeply what it means to follow your heart, and how to do it better and better.

I'm not entirely sure how this topic relates to manifesting intentions (and if there's a "Follow Your Heart" idea I should be talking to about this topic)? But I do still feel some of my attention is on the contrast between following mental structures, rules, and guidelines in order to achieve something vs. a more beingness, attitude, and intuitive approach. It feels like there are conflicting approaches: mind vs. heart, practical/physical vs. intuitive/etheric, structured and direct vs. open, flowing, and surprising.

What do you think? Shall we go exploring this topic area? Maybe, in particular, we could explore how this contrast of approaches relates to intention-work?

II: That sounds like a *fine* exploration for us to co-create and experience together. I'm in. 🤚

Me: OK, so how do you want to structure it? (I'm giggling that I immediately want structure for our exploration.)

II: Yes, that human mind of yours is very entertaining. Sometimes *too* entertaining. ☼

Nevertheless, let us break down our exploration into areas to explore. You're good at keeping us on track for a *full* exploration when I give you the High-level overview first.

Me: OK. I'm already curious to see where you go with this!

II: As am I. ☼

I do like the way you summed up this topic as a contrast. Let's make a list of the contrasts, so your mind can more fully see how it often turns this topic into a right-and-wrong, judgment game.

Mind	Heart
Structured	Open
Physical	Etheric
Practical	Intuitive
Direct	Flow
Obvious	Surprising
Rules	Perspectives
External Action	Internal Attitude
You Say: Doing vs.	Being
I say: Outward Focused vs.	Connected

And now look at how your societal indoctrinations have so often rewarded and applauded the "Mind" side, and often poo-pooed, discredited, or ignored the "Heart" side. There is definitely a lot of fodder here for a right-and-wrong game (which is usually the case if you are experiencing contrast of two poles, rather than a disco-ball effect of *so* many different ways of seeing things).

Me: Seeing this contrast, and feeling how often I have been tug-of-war pulled between these two approaches to life, it makes me wonder: what do I do to integrate all this and not be at war with myself?

II: Exactly the right direction of questioning! It's not about how the social indoctrinations of these two poles came about. It's about how to free yourself to have easy access to *all* the possible approaches.

Me: Aren't we humans built to have preferences for one side, or the other, of this Mind vs. Heart approach?

II: No, not really. That story helps you solidify into an approach you may have already spent years committing to, but humans are really built to be adaptable and to evolve. That's why you have such a developed consciousness (compared to some other types of consciousnesses). You really are explorers, adventurers. And Explorers don't find something and sit on it – they keep exploring. ☺

Me: Good point. It's so easy to get attached to a reference point of "this is the way things are," that I forget how fun it can be to find a new way of doing things. Feels like we're going to be exploring Balance as part of this conversation.

II: Yes: Balance, Exploration, Adventure, Using Your Awareness / Consciousness / Beingness, and Navigating Through Life with Ease, Grace, and a whole lot of Fun!

Me: Sounds like you just laid out our topics of conversation.

II: Indeed! ☺

DAY 38

Me: What do I call this topic area we're starting to explore? We started on the thread of Following Your Heart, but then uncovered this whole theme of contrasting approaches of Mind, etc. vs. Heart et al.

II: We can continue to call it a "Follow Your Heart" topic. The Heart and Mind in Balance, Harmony, and Cooperation together is really the essence of what "Follow Your Heart" ought to mean. Sometimes your society has connected following your heart with dropping all connection to the logical mind. But the truth is, you always have access to both your mind *and* your heart at the same time, every moment. So really, "Follow Your Heart" is like a command you are giving to your mind. The mind still shows up to be of service, but it is in service to the direction of the Heart's greater and more connected Knowing.

Me: OK, so on the topic of "Following Your Heart," how do I create balance?

II: Just as you were discovering in our conversation yesterday, you are imbalanced in a tug-of-war of right vs. wrong when you see all these "life approaches" that I've listed for you as if they are contrasting polar opposites.

So obviously you create Balance in your life approach by learning how to work *Harmoniously* with both seemingly-opposite approaches at the same time.

Me: Sounds like rubbing my tummy and patting my head at the same time. How do I do that when it comes to the Mind, etc. and Heart et al. lists?

THE INTENTION IDEA

[Side Note: I got curious why I was defaulting to calling it Mind, etc. and Heart et al., so I looked up the definition and origins of etc. and et al. Essentially, etc. is used with *things* to mean "and the rest." Et al. is used with other *contributors* to mean "and others." Interesting!]

II: Well, we already talked a little about how to create balance with mind and heart: you let your mind be in service to the Bigger Picture direction that is only fully knowable by the Heart. When we talk about Following your Heart, in the context of manifesting Intentions, we're really talking about tuning in to the Bigger Picture of the whole Intention sea, and putting your thoughts, actions, and explorations in alignment with whatever you are sensing of the Bigger Picture.

Me: OK. Can we go through the rest of the items on the list, and explore how to create Balance for each of them?

II: Sure! For balancing structure and openness, you will need to apply *some* mental structures in order to effectively operate your mind, and to sort and define things you are working with. When you apply structure in an open way, you keep these reference-point structures flexible and able to change when new information comes in. It feels like the floating boundary ropes of a swimming area on a lake: the prescribed safe swimming area is well defined, but it's all connected to one big body of lake water, and the boundary moves with waves or people tugging on it. It can also be completely restructured or dismantled, if that serves the greater good of how the lake space is used.

So too with your mental structures – use them to make your mind (and life) work more effectively for you. But also, allow them to easily shift, change, rearrange, and even disassemble or go away, if it's better that way from a Heart-centered, Bigger Picture perspective.

Me: That analogy makes it seem sooo easy to change a structure. Not at all like the rigid rules and right-and-wrong ways of seeing things I learned in school, and work, and life.

II: Yes, that right-and-wrong game is a doozy for causing fixed, stuck, and rigid ways of being in the world. It's good we are exploring some nuances of how to untangle and navigate your way out of that game, so you can put more energy and focus into the fun, co-creative, exploration games that are also abundant in the Universe.

Me: That sounds *so* much more fun and exciting!

II: I think it is. ☺

DAY 39

Me: OK, so next on the list is physical vs. etheric. How do I find or create balance in these realms?

II: I like that you realized (mid-sentence) that you are *creating* balance, not finding it. Balance isn't some perfect place you get to – like a Shangri-La or utopia. Balance is something you create moment by moment, usually by adjusting your focus of attention so that you aren't over-focused or fixated on one end of a spectrum. Really, the more you are able to hold and explore multiple perspectives at once, the more automatically you will experience Balance in your life. For example, the Universal Big Picture perspective that enjoys *every* experience is always very balanced *and* flexible.

So, for the physical vs. etheric aspect that you experience in life, you can create more balance by being willing to explore and take actions that are physical, *and* explore and take actions that are etheric – or more consciousness-based.

You know very well the warning signs of imbalance on this spectrum: too physical, and not enough etheric, and you end up working really hard to move physical particles and objects around. It may even feel like you're beating your head against a brick wall because you are solidifying the existing physical realities even more when you over-focus on this end of the spectrum.

The other imbalance of too much etheric focus, and not enough physical focus, looks a lot like your stereotypical day-dreamer – always in imagination mode and never taking any physical actions to support their dreams.

To create balance, simply notice what type of "not progress" you are experiencing. If you feel struggle, then do some more etheric work in your consciousness so that you are more connected to the Universal Flow. If you feel good about your Vision, but it seems stagnant, take some kind of action that is in alignment with your Vision.

Me: Simple as that?

II: Yes, it's like riding a bicycle – if you are leaning too much to the right, and about to tip over, then lean more to the left. And of course, no matter which way you lean for your course correction, keep pedaling yourself forward toward your intended destination.

Me: I love your analogies.

DAY 40

Me: Practical vs. intuitive feels like it's related to physical vs. etheric. What's the difference, and how do I create balance on this spectrum?

II: Yes, they are very related. The physical realm is often associated with being practical and working with the seen, visible, or obvious "stuff." Working in the etheric realms does require intuition in order to sense or perceive the unseen, non-physical aspects you are working with. So, in order to create balance in these aspects, you will want to be aware of what perception signals you are paying attention to. If you only see what is physically right in front of you, it would be good to stretch your perception skills. Start looking for, and paying attention to, more subtle aspects in your environment. Keep an openness to synchronicities and stay observant to *everything* that is happening around you. We are all connected. So everything that is happening in this moment *can* be related to your own intended creations. Re-balancing toward more intuitive senses is like having a more peripheral vision awareness of what's going on around you, rather than having a tunnel vision of *only* seeing what's directly in front of you.

To re-balance the other way, toward a more physical realm, you would slow down the distractions of everything around you. Deliberately focus on your intention and only the most obvious things related to your intention.

Me: This feels like eye exercises where you focus on something close, and then scan the wide horizon, shifting back and forth between these two ways of seeing.

II: Yes, similar, but maybe not so much back and forth. Think of it more like a ride on a horse through the country. There are many times you are enjoying experiencing *all* the sights, sounds, and sensations while the horse is carrying you forward. And then there

THE INTENTION IDEA

are also times when you need to have direct, close attention to detail on the horse's reins, or on the trail right in front of you, in order to best navigate the next step. Practical approaches are often needed to navigate the immediate next step, and intuitive approaches often help you understand and sense the Bigger Picture of where you are going in the context of the Whole.

Me: Balance is feeling more and more like having it all.

II: Yes, you *are supposed* to have it all! And you will. We are each here to experience every aspect of the Universe. If you're not experiencing a particular aspect right now, you'll get to it eventually.

Me: So, embrace every viewpoint I come across?

II: Ideally, yes. For now, do your best to appreciate and experience whatever is in front of you and around you.

DAY 41

Me: OK, so how about creating balance in being direct vs. going with the Flow? This is one area where I think I get hung up sometimes. I'm either too directing as I try to force things to fit into my ideal picture of how I think things should be, or I'm too relaxed with more of a laissez-faire attitude of "what will be, will be."

II: Yes, those are good descriptions of what out-of-balance can look like on either end of this spectrum. Let's dive in to creating balance. If you are too directing-oriented, you are probably experiencing a lot of attachment: attachment to the way things already are, and/or attachment to some idea of how you would like things to be. The trick in balancing more toward Flow is to *not* let go of your Intention while you let go of these attachments. One way to do this is to revisit the Bigger Picture feel of your Intention (your intention compass), while you focus on appreciating everything that is. This includes appreciating *all* the possible opportunities you see as available right now.

You can also practice saying "OK" to things. For example, you didn't get the job you interviewed for, and that you thought would be a perfect fit ... say "OK" to that. Or even, things are going great at work, you wouldn't change a thing about it, and you hope it stays the same ... say "OK" to that. Saying "OK" helps you to relax your attachments and judgments, and really *be* with what-is. This non-attached, observant, and appreciative space is an ideal foundation from which to create and attract whatever is next for your intentions.

Now, let's say you're too much in Flow, in a laissez-faire, don't care kind of imbalance. "Just go with the Flow man. Whatever." You know what I mean. Again, reconnect with your Intentions and the details of your intention compass. But in this scenario, you will want to also increase your attitudes and beliefs of "I can do it." Look for your *actionable* next step, and take it. The key is for you to be more of an active participant in the manifestation of your Intentions (and unfoldment of the Universe), and not so much of a passive bystander or witness. Focus your attention on the idea of *co*-creation. Explore the things you can do right now to add to the creation and to support the physical manifestation of your intentions. It doesn't matter how small the actions may seem – do them! Every physical effort is a contribution to the co-creative manifestation of intentions, and *every* effort helps the Universe of intentions move forward.

Me: So, no matter how good it feels to sit and be trusting that it's all being taken care of by the Universe, still get off my ass and do something?

II: Essentially, but let me clarify that your action might be in the etheric realms of consciousness. Co-creative efforts happen in both physical and etheric realms. Just because you experience an imbalance of too much Flow, does not mean the solution is physical action. The solution for re-balancing is more about coming back into alignment as a responsible, equal co-creator with the Universe, rather than expecting everyone else (including the Universe) to work out the details for you. Basically, get your head back into the game, because without your Intention, and sense of direction of what you want to create into the world, the Universal Forces have no Fire with which to create and manifest.

Me: So even just putting my attention back on my intention could be enough to re-balance this aspect?

II: Potentially. Putting attention on your intention while feeling for next steps: definitely.
☺

DAY 42

Me: The next aspect on our list is obvious vs. surprising. This doesn't feel like something I need to balance so much as it is being aware of my preference for the obvious vs. for surprises.

II: Actually, balancing your preferences is just as important as balancing your actions and focus of attention. If you have a strong preference for things to be obvious, you will have an automatic resistance response when you encounter surprises. Likewise, if you have a strong preference for things to be surprising, then you will resist any flows in life that are routine, or cut-and-dried obvious.

To truly experience Flow in all your creating activities, you will need to be OK with obvious perceptions and tasks as well as the delightful or jarring surprises that are all a part of the process of unfoldment.

Me: This makes me think of what my friend Quinn would often say after describing some aspect of how things work: "unless it changes."

II: Yes, being OK with what-is and being OK with things changing are two complementary attitudes that help you create balance in your perceptions of life, and in your reactions and responses to what is happening.

Being appreciative of both the obvious and the surprises helps you maintain a calm center as you navigate life, without being stagnant or stuck.

Me: You've been talking about obvious vs. surprising mostly in the context of perceptions ... feels like that brings us to the next contrast of rules vs. perceptions?

II: Yes, rules are a mental structure – often displayed externally – that represent the desire for obvious perceptions and interactions with life. Rules are an attempt to define and lock in cause-effect relationships. Like, if you do this, then you get rewarded; and if you do that, then you have consequences. Rules can help you navigate large groups, complex interactions, and large amounts of data. But if your focus on rules is too rigid, you won't be able to expand, contract, or otherwise be flexible in the use of the group, interaction, data, or whatever it is you've applied the rule to.

Focusing more on perceptions helps you to be present with what-is, as it is, without a pre-conceived judgment or expectation of how the thing you are perceiving will eventually be sorted, defined, or put to use. Operating from a more perceptual focus puts you in a more exploratory frame of mind. You are willing to see, hear, feel, and experience whatever is there, and so you are more likely to discover new things you would not have noticed if you stayed within the comfort zone of Rules and what is already obvious and known.

The potential imbalance of perceptions is being so focused on experiencing whatever is, that you don't direct the creation of anything new – you are more witness than co-creator or participant. Do you sense the theme? 🖐

Me: Yes, the two sides of this balance coin are becoming more and more clear. So how do I create balance between rules and perceptions?

II: I like the "unless it changes" tagline when you are using rules. That's a nice reminder-to-self to use the rules constructively and be open to any adjustments that help you toward the Bigger Picture Intention.

Frankly you are *way* more likely, as a human, to be out of balance toward rules than you are toward perception. But if you ever find yourself overwhelmed with sensory perception, or lacking a sense of order or direction, then it's a good time for you to decide on some rules for yourself. Write them down for even more sense of structure, or simply say out loud what you are choosing to create.

THE INTENTION IDEA

Affirmations are an example of creating rules for yourself: out of all the available life experiences, you are declaring your direction and intended creation with each affirmation statement you make.

Me: Feels like we get to take all these Universal building block elements and, with one affirmation statement, rearrange all the elements to create a new set of rules and structure.

II: Pretty much. 🙏

DAY 43

Me: OK, next on the list is definitely one I'm eager to explore: external action vs. internal attitude. I feel like societies get easily over-focused on either end of this spectrum – like the classic Western culture "Type A" personality that is always doing, doing, doing and the stereotypical monk on a mountain top who meditates all day. I feel like our work culture attempts to create balance by having spa vacations, tv zone-out time, and do-nothing moments to try to balance very hectic, external-action work weeks. Seems like there is a better way to create balance on a moment-by-moment basis, rather than five days "on" and two days "off."

II: Yes, the balance you have created so far is better than nothing, but it could definitely be a lot better. One of the challenges of your current modes of balancing this aspect is that the opposite of external action that you employ is typically *not* internal attitude work, but rather a numbing, zone-out, feel-nothing approach. If the activities you use to balance external action do not leave you refreshed, renewed, reinvigorated, inspired, and seeing things from an empowered perspective, then you're not really achieving balance. More likely you are hitting a "pause" button and then continuing on again where you left off. When you truly create and achieve balance on this spectrum, you will notice more of a spiraling-upward, collaborative effect. Every moment in action supports your internal attitude explorations, and every moment exploring and creating your internal attitude amplifies your external actions – you get bigger results for the same amount of physical effort.

Me: This feels like an area where I need some more focused practice. Can you give me some examples of how to balance these aspects in daily life?

II: Well for you, since you have such a strong "driver" type of personality (you're often focused on moving things forward and getting things done), balance in everyday life will mean practicing more observant pauses. What I mean by that is *not* pausing and waiting impatiently for things to move forward again, or chewing on thoughts in your mind. Instead, in-between tasks, activities, or projects, and whenever there is a moment to wait for things to move forward again, you can deliberately focus your attention on the sights, sounds, and sensations around you. Really savor what you are experiencing. Sometimes you'll be outside and it will be naturally enjoyable to hear the birds chirping, feel the breeze, and see the plants hanging out in their own plant-time. Sometimes you'll be inside, or surrounded by city, and you are conditioned not to enjoy the sensations of indoors and city life as much as nature. Enjoy it anyway. Appreciate the sounds of people talking, traffic moving, and technology whirring. Look around and notice the colors, shapes, and elements that happen to be in your environment. Don't judge them – just observe them and do your best to appreciate what-is as it is.

Me: Feels like holding the attitude "Everything is all right."

II: Exactly. Allowing yourself the spaciousness to experience what-is opens you up to the Universal Flow, and makes it easier for you to receive your Higher Self's best messages for you right now. Sometimes the message will come as a thought, sometimes it will come through your environment – like a song on the radio, or a person you meet and what they say to you that has a resonance for you.

Internal Attitude has a lot to do with being in tune with *your* flow within the universe – tapping into it and feeling it. *After* you are tuned in, then you can also direct it with the beliefs, affirmations, and attitudes you choose to hold and repeat in your mind.

And then, just to be sure you don't over-focus on the Internal Attitude explorations, check back in with your physical environment and see what next physical actions you can take that are in alignment with your Internal Attitude, and in alignment with where you want to go for the Bigger Picture of your Intentions.

THE INTENTION IDEA

Me: Right now this feels really good. I'm wondering how I'll remember to come back to this place of tuning in to my Flow-within-the-Universe when me and my mind are busy bouncing between and amongst many external actions.

II: The first guideline is to be easy with yourself. Judging yourself for not doing it perfectly, or as well as you'd like, only keeps you stuck in a mental cycle of trying to fix things with external action. So just keep making time – often – to check in with your surroundings wherever you are, and feel, sense, enjoy, and appreciate what-is. The more you do this, the more it will become a natural way of life for you, and you will experience more and more balance and evolutionary forward movement from both your physical, external actions *and* your internal attitude moments. You've got this! ☺

DAY 44

Me: It seems like the last items on the list are one set of contrasts, but with different ways of defining it. Where I would normally call it "Doing vs. Being" (a lot like our last conversation, I notice), instead, you call it "Outward Focused vs. Connected." What's the story here?

II: Yes, it is very much like the last aspects we looked at, especially if you define it as Doing vs. Being. But there is another distinction I'd like for you to be aware of here, in your intention-work and in life. This distinction is explorable in the concepts of outward focus and connection, or being connected.

Let me first describe outward focus and what I mean by it. When you are outwardly focused, you are putting your attention on the scenarios outside of your personal universe – like what are other people doing, what's happening in the environment around you, what do other people think or believe? When in balance, outward focus is in tune with your observant pauses – through all your senses you are drinking in what is happening right now. When out of balance, outward focus has a lot of mind judgments built into it – like how you compare to another person, worry that something dangerous is about to happen in the environment, and constant fretting over what other people might be thinking. Essentially, the out-of-balance outward focus is like a guise, or mask, for what is actually a self-centered focus. All of the attention on outer events and possibilities is really a measurement of potential and real impact to your idea of self.

Me: Sort of like dressing a certain way in order to receive approval, rather than dressing that way because it feels good and serves my higher intention purposes?

II: Yes, that is an example. It's often more subtle though, because a lot of this outward focus lives in your mind and is a result of how you operate your mind. If you let your mind run without guidance from your Higher Self, then you are very likely to end up using the mind to always be calculating for your own sense of safety, survival, and self-preservation. Sadly the "self" the mind is trying to preserve at this point is not the real "You" – it's the identity the mind has fabricated as its idea of you. *You* are so much more, beyond your mind and your body. The real You can direct your will and change your focus of attention. And this real You is the true master of your life course – when you tune into it.

So, an out-of-balance outward focus could be overly focused on all the stuff going on around you (most obvious). Or, you could be overly focused on your own mental chatter and internal judgments of what's seemingly going on (not as obvious, but more prevalent).

Me: Sounds like "monkey-mind" – it keeps chattering away, with more and more vicious talk, trying to grab my attention.

II: Yes, that is another way of looking at it. But I don't want you to just label it "monkey-mind," think it's bad or wrong, and try to get rid of it. Seeing the whole picture of these aspects, and how to balance them, will give you a smoother integration and more graceful life practice, with less propensity for right-and-wrong games.

Me: OK, so how about the connected side of the coin?

II: Being connected means you are in Flow with the Universe and everything in it. You are in harmony. You show up as the real you, providing your unique gifts and perspectives. And you are enjoying, appreciating, and collaborating with all the many other varieties of perspectives and creations you encounter as you move through life. There is little resistance to what-is – maybe just some boundaries that define your You-ness and your creations. And, the boundaries are resulting from your decisions and intentions of what to create, rather than from reactions or attempts to protect.

THE INTENTION IDEA

Me: Feels a bit like your defined swimming area on a lake again.

II: Yes, that's really an ideal analogy for setting boundaries since it's flexible but still well-defined.

Me: Your description of being connected sounds like a pretty ideal way to live. How could it possibly be out-of-balance?

II: It is rare in humans. But, if you ever find yourself without a sense of your Higher Self and your unique contributions to the world, then you have probably gone too far (for the purposes of your human life) in your exploration of the Universe's One-ness. You are here to express, create, and explore your unique interests. When you do your creating and exploring in harmony with the whole Universe, then you feel connected, and you and the whole Universe expand and evolve together. When you try to do your creating and exploring as if you are an isolated being whose experiences are all your own, and not to be shared, then you lose connection and move more toward the outward-focused mask covering your own attempts at "self" preservation.

Me: This feels like an area where perfect balance is needed — like now we're riding a unicycle instead of a bicycle, so it's harder to stay in the middle without also moving forward.

II: Yes, that's a good analogy. ☺ On a bicycle you have more surface tension with the ground, so you can maintain your balance more easily. On a unicycle there is only one wheel's surface tension, so it requires more focus of your attention on this aspect in order to balance. Plus, you don't have handlebars, so you're really stepping up your responsibility and actions to keep your balance.

And really, you are balancing between an ego-centric perspective and a "contributing to the Whole" perspective. Your society has often called the opposite of ego-centric approaches "Oneness," but you'll notice in my description of Connection that you explicitly do *not* lose your sense of Higher Self purpose while you are harmoniously connecting with the Universe.

If you look more closely at what harmony is, it really is unique voices, tones, or vibrations, that play well together. If you try to experience "oneness" as if you lose your unique voice, and are just a monotone part of a whole, then you are trying to create everyone playing the same note together. That got boring real fast, and that's why we are enjoying so *many* varied perspectives and ways of being. But, without connection and playing together in harmony, our unique voices and interests feel pretty chaotic at times. That's OK to experience too, we're just ready, as a Universe, to evolve into more and more harmonious co-creative games.

Me: Wow, this connectedness feels *very* Big Picture!

II: Indeed it is. And the more you allow yourself to sense (in any ways that you sense) how your unique contributions play in harmony with the Universe, then you are re-balancing toward an ideal amount of connectedness with the ideal application of outward-focus.

Me: What are some practical things I can do to balance this aspect?

II: Good question. One thing you can do is ask your questions that help you focus on the Bigger Picture of benefitting others. For any action you are about to make, especially if you feel a niggling sense of doubt about it, or like you need to protect yourself in some way, then ask: "Does this action benefit others, and does everyone win?"

Following the general intention-work guidance we've discussed should also help you keep balanced on this aspect. If you have any doubts, you can look for ways you might be trying to protect yourself. Do some inner explorations to uncover any hidden beliefs, or intentions, you might have taken on that are preventing you from fully showing up as you and being fully connected and in harmony with everyone and everything around you.

THE INTENTION IDEA

Me: That sounds like a pretty deep, complicated inner exploration.

II: It doesn't have to be. Start with your tools for removing obstacles and see where it takes you. ☺

DAY 45

Me: I'm going to take Intention Idea's suggestion and use the removing obstacle questions to explore how I might be trying to protect myself. I feel like I'm protecting myself with respect to money. I'm especially aware of this idea that money always involves give and take. I'm worried I'll be over-taken from, or I'll over-give, and in either case I will be without the resources I need for my own survival (there's the idea that I need to protect my "self!"). What follows are my journal writings as I use the "Rock Questions" for removing obstacles to explore this a bit further.

1. What's really going on here?
Give and take social indoctrinations and stories of imbalance. Money rules that make it "us vs. them" or "me vs. them." People abusing others and trying to over-take. Not a lot of harmony and collaborating to create more – more like trying to take from what-is. There's the idea that money is a limited resource pool, and the only way to have more is to take from others – no blueprints for how to collaborate to create more money for everyone. How *does* that work? Bitcoin? That's still based on limited supply. The war machine economy is based on destruction and beliefs that rally people to "invest" more time and money into inventions for it.

2. Why is it important?
A lot of social interactions and structures are built on money, so how do we transform to a collaborative game? Money is used for living with others in society. The only other known option is being off grid. You're either in or you're out.

3. What are the feelings and sensations involved?
Fear, tension, worry, greedy, wanting what's mine, wanting to grab it and take it in order to be safe. Not-enoughness.

4. What are the thoughts, ideas, and beliefs, especially the ones on repeating loops around this topic?

So many money beliefs! There's no good way around this. There has to be a better way. I can't do it. I'm stuck. It's not mine to solve. *It's bigger than me.*

Ironically "it's bigger than me" keeps me from seeing and being connected with the Big Picture. With this belief, I'm establishing that money is a part of the Universe that's separate from me – not in my part of the Universe, not part of the Universe *I* collaborate with.

Oooh, there's a good intention statement!
I collaborate with money.

DAY 46

Me: OK, so I tried exploring this area where I feel I'm trying to protect myself – money. And the questions for removing obstacles were amazing for helping me explore and uncover hidden beliefs, and aspects about money, and how I try to protect myself – or my sense of self.

But, maybe because it's such a big, convoluted topic (or so I believe), I still have some confusion about how to integrate this Bigger Picture perspective. I mean, how *do* I collaborate with money?

II: Yes, you (of course) picked a topic with a lot of aspects to it – all the more for you to explore and play with. It's good that you uncovered some of the social indoctrinations and beliefs that keep you separate from others when you are working with money. As I've said before, just being *aware* of the obstacle, or mind-made limitation, will help you to navigate around it and/or turn it off. It's OK if your integration of this awareness doesn't have an immediate Aha! effect to it – sometimes it will be a light bulb or flash of lightning moment, and sometimes it will be a more gradual dawn.

As you continue to contemplate how to "collaborate with money," you will find answers specific to you that help you achieve the perfect balance of your own Higher Self perspectives – both connected and outward focused.

Me: Dang, I was really hoping you'd just give me the answer. You know – quick, easy steps to solve my over-focus on protecting my self when it comes to money.

II: It's just like your qigong instructor said: "The magic is in the journey, the destination is just an illusion because you're never really done."

THE INTENTION IDEA

Me: So, keep exploring thoughts and ways for collaborating with money?

II: Yes, this is *your* magical journey, enjoy it! 🖐

* * *

Me: I thought I'd share with you the mind map I drew about collaborating with money after this conversation with Intention Idea. To me, it feels like a nice compass for understanding and relating four major ways I see for collaborating with money.

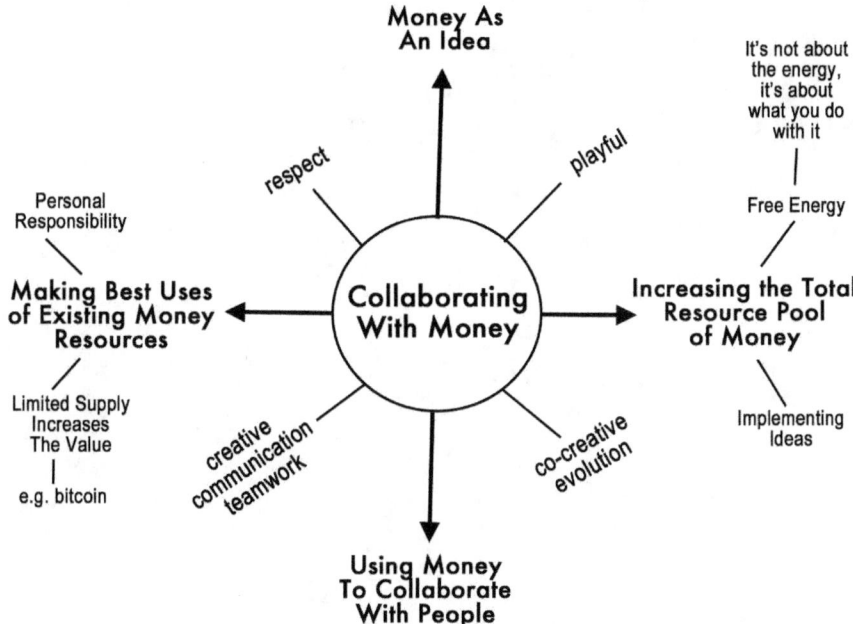

After drawing this mind-map, I happened across an abundance visualization where you imagine yourself peacefully floating in the endless ocean. Then you imagine the ocean is whatever you've been feeling lack of (like money), and you are floating in it, seeping it into your body through all your pores.

THE INTENTION IDEA

After doing the visualization, and looking at my mind map again, I felt a peace about collaborating with money. This phrase came to mind, and it summed up the experience (and the intention) nicely for me:

Money is like the Ocean: There's more than enough for everyone to create with.

DAY 47

Me: I feel like my own magical journey around collaborating with money has taken us right into the next topic area for Following Your Heart: Exploration. What does exploration have to do with Following Your Heart?

II: Yes, you are right on track in your own personal explorations to be a perfect example, or working subject, for our conversation. Everything is as it's supposed to be – and if it isn't, it will still work out perfectly. ☺

As you've noticed (a little bit), when you enter into exploration mode with a more open, curious, and wondering mind, you are creating a quieter space in which to listen to the current guidance of your Higher Self, your Heart. As you explore a topic, like you are currently exploring collaborating with money, new perspectives and insights pop into your awareness, and new resources of information show up to support your exploration.

Me: Like how that book about visualizing your perfect weight had a visualization about abundance being like the ocean, and that fed perfectly into the summary of my mind map of collaborating with money?

II: You know it! And the more and longer you stay in this open, curious, exploration mode, the more you will attract new insights and resources. It's like all the pieces of a puzzle being magnetized to you so that you can sort them into an order that makes the most sense for your life.

Me: It feels a bit like the Direction phase of intention-work and the act of creating an intention compass.

II: Yes, the two activities go hand-in-hand. You must be in exploration mode in order to build an intention compass, and when you are in exploration mode it's only natural that you will be guided by your Higher Self (and Heart) in directions of exploration and understanding that serve your Highest Purposes.

Me: Sounds like a win-win.

II: That's the way the Universe likes to roll. ☺

Me: So how else does exploration fit with Following Your Heart? As I look at our list of contrasts it seems like you have to be more in an exploratory mode (rather than a defining mode) in order to access most of the aspects on the heart side of the list. Like being open, intuitive, experiencing Flow, surprises, and perspectives – all that seems very in tune with exploration. Where is all this Follow Your Heart exploration stuff taking us?

II: Following Your Heart and exploration will always take you to greater expansion: more evolution and more understanding of self, of environment, of intentions, and of the Universe. The opposite direction is contraction, which locks you in to definitions and ways of being. Definition is fine in moderation – to help give you stable reference points from which to leap off of and create new things. If you ever feel stagnant, stuck, or frustrated, then you need more exploration and following your heart in order to experience more growth.

Me: That makes sense. So, are intentions a part of exploration, growth, and following your heart?

II: Intentions are *absolutely* involved with exploration, growth, and Following Your Heart! Through intentions, you create new experiences to explore, and you help the Universe to grow and expand into new territories of experience. Your Heart is a direct access point to the You – the Higher Self You – that is fully in tune

THE INTENTION IDEA

with the Whole Universe, operating in harmony with everyone and everything. When we talk about Following Your Heart, we're exploring more and more aspects for how you co-create in harmony with the Universe. We're exploring the nuances of showing up as You, bringing your unique gifts to the World, and how your uniqueness collaborates and co-creates with all the other uniquenesses. It's like one big finger-painting party where we all get messy together, enjoy expressing ourselves individually, and explore the effects of each contribution to the whole montage, or mural, or whatever medium we are painting on and playing on together.

Me: That gives me an impression of Earth as our butcher paper, and every live being is doing some kind of finger-painting on it. Some dries and stays, and some gets washed away or covered up.

II: Yes, that's a good visual, especially because it feels so playful. If you look at every act in life as if it were your (or their) playful finger-painting exploration, then it's OK if it's not "perfect" or always in harmony with everyone. It's all a part of the fun exploration of living, cohabitating a planet together, and finding both dissonance and harmony as you co-create. It's all OK, and you're never really done with the painting – you can always add more paint. ☺

Me: There's something about finger-painting that feels so freeing and playful. It's not a very precise mode of art (at least not for me!).

II: Yes, and exploration and following your Heart is not meant to be precise. To discover new things, ideas, perspectives, or ways of seeing things, you may want to live with more wild abandon (at least with respect to the final outcome). Just enjoy the sensory experiences as you create and explore, create and explore.

Me: At what point do I start to add definition to the explorations?

II: Only when it amuses you or feels richly satisfying. Like if you are finger-painting, and you want to define your current masterpiece as a "cat," then do it. If you don't want to label it as a picture of anything, then don't, and keep painting or enjoying it simply as it is. Even if you do define it as a picture of a cat, you may want to keep exploring it within that definition. What kind of cat is it, or what other aspects of this cat picture do you want to explore? Or, take that "cat" definition off and see the picture completely differently. The whole point of exploration is to keep you constantly tuned in to the subtle energetic messages of your Heart and Higher Self. Defining things tends to put you more into a rigid, mental state. So even if you feel called to define something you've been exploring, keep *exploring* it! Stay open to your definitions changing, the thing you're looking at changing, and *you* changing. We are in a living, evolving, ever-changing Universe, so exploration mode is one of your best skills for riding the many waves of change and evolution.

DAY 48

Me: Next on the topics you laid out for us is adventure. Seems like that goes hand in hand with exploration. What's the difference?

II: Adventure brings in even more of a sense of appreciation for what-is and what you are exploring. If you have a "sense of adventure," or an adventurous attitude, then you are pre-dispositioning yourself to appreciate and enjoy the changing and unexpected landscape you are exploring (whether that landscape is external or internal). Adventure also has an element of fun to it – like when you are enjoying a new and delightful surprise. Some people may have defined themselves as "not adventurous" if they like to feel safe, comfortable, in control, and "in the know" of what is happening and what is about to happen.

Truth is, life and all living beings are adventurous. Only the mind-space has the illusion of control and safety. You, as a living being, are *always* on an adventure with unknowns and delightful surprises.

Me: What do I do if I'm feeling particularly not-adventurous, and I'm craving or clinging to my mental sense of safety and comfort?

II: Well, one thing you could do is take a Higher perspective view of your life. Recognize and appreciate all the ways you really haven't "*known*" what is going to happen, and how you have always figured out how to create some kind of outcome that is acceptable to you.

If you're feeling really "clingy" for safety and security, go ahead and create a sense of safety for yourself in whatever way you feel you need. Though, I feel I should remind you that your ultimate security and sense of safety comes from knowing who you are as a Higher Self and powerful creator. If you need reminding of that Higher Self perspective, it might be a good time to go back to the questions for removing obstacles and exploration of what aspect or aspects of your "self" you feel you are needing to protect.

Me: I feel like if we're going to talk about adventure, I should include my story of "Adventure Day" that my partner, Dan, and I created and use when we might otherwise be in a mind-freakout.

II: Yes, that's a great story to tell here to illustrate the value of adventure, both as a practice of directing your attention and for re-framing events that don't seem to be going "your way." ☺

Me: OK. So, Dan and I started creating a weekly "Adventure Day," when we would deliberately get out of our daily routines at home and go spend some time in nature. Usually we go hiking, and we now have some preferred hikes, but when we started Adventure Day we were new to this location and we focused most of our adventures on exploring areas of nature we hadn't been to before. Just getting in the car and heading out to our destination, we usually announce to each other, "Oh boy! Adventure Day!" and it puts us in a happy mood, expectant of delightful surprises. Even if it's one of our usual favorite hikes we default to now, we still expect delightful surprises, because we really don't know what our experience will be like out there today, and we expect it will be fun.

Here's the twist on Adventure Day and how it came about. We were travelling from Portland, Oregon to Orlando, Florida to help deliver an Avatar Course when our flight through Salt Lake City got cancelled and we were re-routed through JFK airport in New York. That put us into Orlando six hours later than we had originally planned. While I was initially bummed to miss spending time with my friend that we had pre-arranged, Dan turned to me with bright eyes and a lot of excitement and said, "Oh boy! Adventure Day!"

We both laughed, and then relaxed into an attitude of adventure, wondering who we might meet and what we might experience with this change of plans. Nothing overly exceptional happened on the rest of our trip, but we were relaxed and enjoying our travel, and everything worked out fine for getting to the Avatar Course on time.

Actually, I guess you could say something exceptional happened, because it left a deep and enjoyable impression of re-framing a change of plans as an Adventure Day. It's a phrase we still use often – both for our deliberate adventures and for the surprise plot twists that sometimes happen in our plans.

I feel like Adventure Day puts me into a more relaxed, open, intuitive, and "in the Flow" attitude – like I'm on vacation and don't need to rush, or push, to make things happen a certain way.

II: Yes, the sense of adventure has all those aspects built into it, and perhaps most especially the relaxation of expectations. In order to follow your Heart as you navigate life, it's important that you stay open to new ways of seeing things, different ways of doing things, and appreciating outcomes that are unexpected.

DAY 49

Me: You mentioned "using your Awareness / Consciousness / Beingness" as an aspect of Following Your Heart for us to explore. This feels like a complex topic already. Can you start by explaining what you mean by this phrase?

II: Sure! I put all these terms together to help you understand the *experience* I'm trying to convey through these word concepts. There are more words we could also use, but let me see if I can get the point across without adding more terms.

When you are in your mind, and operating your mind to perceive and make sense of your world, you can also be aware of parts of you that are not the mind. Some might call this "not-mind" a pure Awareness: the Beingness that perceives and creates, without the mental structures of sorting, defining, judging, labeling, and reasoning. Some might call it Consciousness, referring to the aware part of you that directs the mind, makes decisions, and activates your Will in order to create action. And some might call this aspect pure Beingness: beyond thoughts, beyond doingness, beyond identities and memories – simply *BE*-ing, presence with what-is.

Me: This feels similar to how you've described Higher Self and the Heart I'm following.

II: Yes. This aspect of Following Your Heart is about using all of your resources and faculties in order to access, experience, and operate in the world as the *real* you – the Pure Awareness Beingness that is not your mind or body, but that is so linked to these human aspects that you can direct, control, use, and navigate life with the mind and body.

Me: Is this like a Soul?

THE INTENTION IDEA

II: That term often has a lot of indoctrination baggage with it, so I prefer to reference your Higher Self.

The important thing here is not the term, not the definition, and not the conceptual understanding. The important thing here to really *get* is the experience.

Me: How does anyone "get" this experience? It feels like human society is so geared toward using the body and/or mind – and therefore identifying with the body and/or mind – that it's rare to have an opening to explore the Higher Self.

II: Yes, there is a lot of over-identification with body and mind, in place of experiencing the Higher Self. But there are also *many* avenues for opening to and experiencing the Real You. Meditation is an increasingly more well-known way to connect with and experience your Higher Self. Art, journaling, and channeled writing are other ways. Some body movement practices, when paired with a spiritual or etheric intent, can also help you to experience your Higher Self.

Perhaps, the simplest way is for you to keep following your intuition. Every time you pause, listen to, and follow your inner sensation of "knowing" which way to go in any decision, you are connecting with and operating as your Higher Self, Pure Awareness, Pure Beingness.

Me: Does that mean I'm not connected to my Higher Self when I'm not following my intuition?

II: It's not that you are disconnected – because your Higher Self is *always* there, available, and part of you. It's more that you are using your mind to turn off the perceptions of your Higher Self.

Me: Like putting my fingers in my ears while singing la-la-la-la la-la-la?

II: Yes, but you usually do it with a more serious attitude. If you *were* more playful about it, you'd be more likely to uncover your ears and listen again. ☺

Me: OK, so how do I *use* my Awareness / Consciousness / Beingness in the context of Following my Heart?

II: As I said, listening to and following your Intuition is a good place to start. The more your actions (and thoughts) are in alignment with your intuition, the more in tune you are with the Universe and your Higher Self – your Heart. It's not that there is one ideal path of destiny for you to follow in life, but there is a natural Flow – a sense of order – that you as a Pure Awareness, Higher Self Being put into motion at one point in time. Fighting, resisting, or restricting that Flow leads to struggle, suffering, and contraction. Tapping into that Flow, going with it, playing with it, co-creating its next direction – all of those actions result in joy, ease, grace, and enjoyment of life.

Me: That's a strong vote for following my intuition! I'd much rather enjoy my life than experience struggle.

II: Well, it's OK if you sometimes choose struggle and not listening. If you didn't have the choice available to listen or not to listen, the action of listening wouldn't be quite as delicious.

Me: Like how good it feels to breathe deeply and freely after holding my breath for a while?

II: Yes. The interesting thing is that humans often want to test that choice: to experience constraint and then Flow, constraint and then Flow. For whatever reason, human life seems to have a fascination with that contrasting experience, so I'd suggest you just be OK with it when it happens. Take it as a plot twist, or adventure day, and keep moving forward toward the intentions and life you prefer to experience next.

THE INTENTION IDEA

Me: No Biggie?

II: Well, as a human, some things will seem like a pretty big deal – like life threatening events. But as a Pure Awareness / Consciousness / Beingness that endures beyond a single human life, most events are simply "interesting," "curious," and some version of enjoyable.

Me: That feels like a pretty bold statement that our Awareness / Consciousness / Beingness endures beyond a single human lifetime. What if someone doesn't believe in more than one lifetime?

II: Then that is their belief, and they will construct their life according to their beliefs. Unless it changes.

Me: Like unless they die and have a different experience than what they expected, and so they change their belief?

II: It could happen. ☺

Me: If our beliefs create our experiences, how could someone experience something outside of what they believed was possible?

II: Your beliefs create your experiences within *your* field of influence – like your attitude, state of mind, your actions, and your body. But there are also fields of influence within the Universe that are outside of your "belief jurisdiction." For example, what you believe about others impacts *your* experience of others, but does not necessarily impact their experience of themselves.

Me: We're back to that collage of beliefs, all interacting and affecting each other and the Bigger Picture experience again, huh?

II: Yes, and it's a valuable analogy when you are considering how to

Follow Your Heart.

Me: How so?

II: When you open to listening more – listening to your intuition, your Higher Self, and your Heart's guidance – you are also likely to hear more of *all* the sounds and promptings of the Universe. You are not alone, not the only Awareness / Consciousness / Beingness operating in the Universe. We are many Powerful Beings Co-Creating and Playing together. As you listen to your own inner promptings, you will eventually also want to listen to, and coordinate with, other people's Heart Intuitions in harmony with your own.

DAY 50

Me: I feel like I'm still settling in to the experience of what you said about there being many Powerful Beings co-creating and playing together. It's starting to feel like every conversation, every interaction, is an opportunity to listen to the Universe and contribute to the creation of experiences we are all having.

For example, last night I was talking with a friend who was very much in his mind while he was evaluating some possible next steps for what he wants to create on his career path. He was so involved in his own "mind-stuff" and career direction decisions that he didn't have much attention available for me and *my* mind-stuff. If I look at our conversation from just my viewpoint, as if I were the only Pure Awareness Being on the planet, then it's easy for me to feel a bit disappointed when I'm not getting encouraging responses, or interest and attention, on what's important to me (and my mind). But when I view our conversation as two Powerful Beings co-creating experiences together, then it feels like *everything* my friend says and does – even when he's lost in his mind-stuff – is contributing some kind of amazingness to my journey of experiences. And vice versa, anything I say or do is contributing to his experiences of life.

Somehow, something so simple as a conversation suddenly feels more like a sacred exploration of two Powerful Beings supporting each other on their journeys. Or as Ram Dass says, "We are all just walking each other home."

Am I alone in this revelation? Or how do I really convey this profound experience? (That's really my question).

II: You don't need to even *think* about how to convey the experience. The magic of Following Your Heart is that every person who *does* follow their heart will have their own experiences, unique to them, that reveal more and more of the Sacred, Profound, and Connected experiences as a Powerful Being Co-Creating with other

Powerful Beings. It's a natural unfoldment that comes with tapping in, and tuning in, to your Heart and to the Universe.

Me: Sounds like I'm leading us right into the next topic you had queued for us: navigating through life with ease, grace, and a whole lot of fun.

II: Yes, all the topics around Following Your Heart have a nice Flow together – of course! And, as you are starting to see from the sacredness you felt in your conversation with your friend last night, Following Your Heart leads to a natural evolution, unfoldment, and progression of navigating *all* of life's experiences with ease, grace, and fun - enjoyment!

Me: It's feeling more and more like I'm in an orchestra, or one continuous jazz jam session, that is constantly adjusting and morphing based on which players are joining in at any given moment.

II: Yes, that's essentially what is always happening in the Universe, and a great attitude to take that comes naturally with this analogy. We are all, always, contributing our perspectives, vibrations, attitudes, and experiences to this thing called life. If you choose to view all your life experiences as one great big jam session, then any disharmony, changes in tempo, solos, key changes, or any other kind of "plot twist" is part of the fun of co-creating together. You learn to adapt, find new ways of creating harmony, find new enjoyments of dissonance, and roll with whatever happens as you lean in to your own melodies you want to bring forth.

Me: You make it sound so easy!

II: Yes and no. If you've ever seen or participated in *any* kind of jam session (musical or otherwise), you'll know that all the players imbue a calm relaxedness while also attentive to where the whole group is going. They make it look easy because of their relaxed attitude. And they are able to handle all the challenges of constantly changing

THE INTENTION IDEA

group directions because they are showing up with all of their proficiencies, coupled with a willingness to work together.

Me: And if something doesn't work in the group's dynamic or jam session results?

II: Then laugh at the experience that wasn't as desired, learn from it how to adapt better together, identify the areas where you need to practice and increase your own proficiencies, and above all else: Keep Going! ☺

DAY 51

Me: One of the things our conversation has me thinking about and contemplating is my intention that "I am living the life of my dreams." There's something about that particular phrase of words and the feel of that intention that a) helps me to appreciate and feel grateful for all the parts of my life that really are as awesome as I have dreamt it to be, and b) gets me thinking about what the life of my dreams really looks like and how I want to shape it next. Right now, I feel a *lot* of gratitude for where I live, my partner Dan and our relationship, my work (my day job) where I get to apply my mind in useful ways that are appreciated, and my time writing and conversing with you. When I look for what might be missing in this life of my dreams – current rendition – I come back to money. But, now I have more clarity about my dreams about money. It's never been my dream to win the lottery, or inherit a lot of money, or to own a lot of stuff. I *do* feel my dream of earning more than enough money to live comfortably, travel, and do what I want when I want. It's also my dream to earn that money by providing something of value that lots of people really appreciate and enjoy.

It feels like a lot of people are searching for something like this now – wanting to be "solopreneurs," working for themselves, doing work that they love, being more creative, and not being bound by rigid corporate structures (or rigid money structures for that matter). How do I navigate through this transition of our whole society from a corporate work system to a do-what-you-love system? And how do I allow it to be, really, *soooo* good of a life that it feels like I'm living the life of my dreams?

II: It's beautiful that you are hearing your Heart's Ultimate Wish for creating the life of your dreams – no limitations on how awesome and amazing it can be, or on how much greater and awesomer it will keep evolving into as you grow. And it's OK that you are bumping up against some beliefs, indoctrinations, societal expectations, and general feelings of constraint as you pursue this path of living the life of your dreams. Perhaps if you did not first taste some struggle and resistance on your journey, the life of your dreams would not taste as sweet as it does now?

Me: You mean, like how much *more* I savor and revel in living in the Pacific Northwest after being away from it for the eight years I lived in Dallas, Texas? I *definitely* don't take it for granted, and it does seem extra special and delicious having experienced the contrast.

II: Yes, that's a great example. Perhaps the next time you are experiencing a contrast, or seeming limitation, you can remember this example. You can choose to view the resisted experience as the strength training, or in this case "savoring and gratitude training," that increases your appreciation of what you prefer.

Me: That gives a whole new meaning to resistance training. It's like I'm practicing resisting an experience so that I can more fully embrace my preferred experience.

II: Yes, but it only works when you also dip your toes in and allow yourself to experience the thing you are resisting. If you resist eating an apple, then allow yourself to experience it and actually take a bite, then when you return to eating your preferred oranges, they taste all the sweeter because you actually tasted something different. So, you're not really *staying* in resistance.

Me: It's more like "resistance-to-experience training"?

II: Yes, that's it.

Me: So, every time I allow myself to really experience worries about money, or doing work that isn't really doing *everything* that I love, I'm doing "resistance-to-experience training" that is going to make the experience of earning money doing what I love that much sweeter?

THE INTENTION IDEA

II: Yes. In your specific case, you have had times in your life when you had a lot of money flowing to and through you, and also times when you have *only* done what you loved (though often with money worries during those times). At this junction of time and space, you are earning money, enjoying your work, and creating time to do what you love. It tastes sweeter, doesn't it?

Me: It would taste better if there were more money and it *all* came from doing only what I love.

II: Yes, I feel your intention, and I know you are on the long hike of creating that intention. Now remember to *enjoy* every aspect of the journey along the way.

Me: I feel a bit like the stereotypical spoiled kid, and I just want to whine, "but why can't I have what I want now?!?"

II: Because I said so? ☺ More likely because you said so. You set it up to co-create in human form on earth, with a bunch of other co-creators and *some* restrictions on how manifestation works in the physical realms. The most important part of your experience of this manifestation journey is that you enjoy yourself, appreciate what-is, and be who you want to be where you are now. Don't wait for *any* end result in order to be happy and enjoy life. Experience the ease, grace, and *fun* of co-creating exactly where you are right now!

DAY 52

Me: I have another question about navigating life with ease, grace, and fun. I'm aware that sometimes I can fool myself into thinking I'm co-creating with the flow of the Universe when, really, I'm resisting addressing a limitation in my mind, or delaying stretching past a comfort zone. You know, like saying "I'm just going with the flow," or "this must be the way of the Universe right now," instead of deliberately holding my intention and taking action to make it happen. It feels like such an easy (and common) way to deceive myself and lull myself into a non-driving, not-moving-forward complacency. It's so easy to just blame my lack of results on "not good Universal timing."

But here's the flip side of this phenomenon. I think I'm *so* worried that I might fool myself into complacency and not doing my part to get things done, that I'm not really trusting the Flow of the Universe and relaxing into the rhythm of Universal timing for my creations. I think this might be why I've had a tendency to try to "push the river" to make things happen – just to make sure I'm not slacking off, or in an illusion of expecting things to happen with no effort.

How do I find the balance here, and really *know* if it's best to pause, wait, do something else, chill out, back off a bit, and simply enjoy what-is, or when it's time to look at the obstacles, find a way around them, and really drive and push forward to make something happen?

U: From a Universal Energy perspective, you never need to push. That's a very mind-oriented response and approach to manifesting. Heart-centered intention-work will always have a sense of intuitive Flow to it. You will intuit a Flow to look at an obstacle and contemplate ways around it. You will intuit an action to take, or where to put your attention, and you will connect more and more dots of a Bigger Picture that helps everything move forward and grow naturally. The mind would like to have it all figured out as if life were a machine you program, power-up, and set in motion. But life is an unfolding, interactive, fluid chaos of creation that does not move forward like a machine chomping through data. It grows like a vine pushing out new growth in the spring, reaching for additional plants and resources to co-create with, Flowering, Fruiting, experiencing the fullness of its creation, and returning back to the quiet stillness of the dormant season, gathering new resources to begin again. Let your life, your intentions, your projects and co-creations, and your whole navigation of all of life follow this more natural flow of the Universe. With this approach, you won't have to worry or check in on your measurements of relaxation vs. stretching.

Put another way, if you aren't inspired to act, you must need something else first. Maybe you *need* rest, nourishment, and quiet time. Maybe you need to explore other perspectives and a different way of doing things. Maybe you need to stew in a resisted experience or limitation for a bit, before you feel inspired to dive in, address it, and experience it fully. Whatever you are experiencing, it really is OK. You will always learn and grow from everything on your path, and every experience is valuable for the entire Universe's Evolution.

So, let go of your judgments, your measurements, and your expectations about going from point A to point B in a straight line. Allow yourself to enjoy *everything* on your journey, allow your path to meander for even *more* experiences, and *know* that it's not important to reach an end goal. It's important to be present and appreciative of every experience you create.

DAY 53

Me: Here's another question for you about navigating life with ease and grace (and OK, a whole lot of fun). I've been noticing lately how much my mind tries to establish cause and effect, in order to determine what to do next. Like in my role at work, I'm always looking at our numbers to see which of our marketing efforts resulted in more sales. But also, in my personal life, I'm often wondering which of the things I've changed has caused my current results. I want to know where to continue my efforts, or which efforts to stop if I'm not getting results.

Lately I've been realizing that it may not be *one* thing that is causing my results, but *all* the things I'm doing that are causing results. How do I discern which actions are working best in my personal harmony of actions, and which should be stopped or changed?

II: You found the key to your answer when you connected the dots and realized you have a "personal harmony of actions." Just as the Universe seeks harmony of experiences – all the individual contributions working together to create a more harmonious, enjoyable Whole Picture – so does your personal life, and *all* of your many projects, mirror this relationship of individual contributions to a greater harmony of the Whole.

Me: The microcosm mirrors the macrocosm?

II: Indeed. So if you want to know how to make decisions about starting, stopping, altering, or continuing any individual contributors to an effect you are working to achieve, you will be best served to look at the Bigger Picture, get a sense of how it sounds, and then listen to the individual component and how its contributions are impacting the harmony.

Me: I'm not a singer, or at least not versed in singing harmony, so this feels pretty challenging to do. Can you break it down for me a little more?

II: Yes of course. Let's take a real-life example to work with.

Me: OK, losing weight has been on my mind lately. I've gained some weight in the last two years and haven't been able to lose what I've gained (yet). I'm pretty sure I gained the weight from stress at work, and/or hormonal changes (pre-menopause), and/or winter comfort food eating (although I've cleaned up my diet a lot in the last three months with little effect).

I've been trying a lot of different things: I've been improving my work-life to make it less stressful and more enjoyable. I've been working with a naturopath to supplement with herbs to balance my hormones. I've been eating healthier. I was running three to four times a week, until I injured my knee, but I'm still walking every day. And I started listening to a night-time guided visualization for achieving my ideal body.

On that last new action, the guided visualization, I have noticed that I haven't been as hungry the last few days, and it made me wonder if the visualization is working. But I've also noticed how calm and centered I've been feeling, and I'm wondering if that's from my explorations with you, or from the guided visualization that has a lot of relaxation exercises in it, or from my work being that much better from all the changes I've made lately. Or all of the above?

II: Yes, perfect example of how busy the mind can get while trying to figure out what's happening, in order to better control it, rather than simply *enjoying* what is happening and being OK with it all, as it is. ☺

So, in this example, the Bigger Picture is the vision you have of yourself in your ideal body, doing the activities you love doing, feeling comfortable in your own skin, and really enjoying how your body feels. You have this Bigger Picture pretty well defined from the work you've already done with the guided visualization.

Now let's take one of the individual components and "listen" to it to hear how it is contributing to the harmony of your Bigger Picture.

Me: How about exercise? I'm wondering why I hurt my knee running, and what I should be doing for exercise.

II: OK, perfect! When you "listen" to this component of exercise, what do you hear? How is it manifesting for you now? What do you feel when you contemplate exercise? What is happening?

Me: Well, I immediately hear the thought that I should be exercising more if I want to lose weight. But, I feel a bit hesitant about exercising. When I was all gung-ho about running on the trampoline for 15 minutes three times a week, and walking every day at lunch, I seem to have injured my knee from running, and I'm not sure that I had much, if any, weight loss. I like the evening walks I do with Dan, and our weekend hikes. I like the idea I got from *The Gabriel Method* to do some sprinting in my walks, like I'm being chased, so my body knows I need to be thin in order to outrun my "chaser". I like the little bits of yoga I've been doing, but I haven't gotten myself into a regular routine of it yet. Overall, I can feel my mistrust: that any gentle exercise I do is not going to have an effect. But, at the same time, I'm worried about injuring myself if I try to do too much. Oh! And I can also hear in my contemplations the story of my friend who has lost a lot of weight with her main exercise of *lots* of walking and counting her steps, but I'm not thrilled by the idea of counting steps.

II: Can you feel all the push and pull in your contemplation of exercise? There are some good feelings that pull you toward exercise options that are perfect for you, and then there are resistance feelings that push experiences away.

Me: So, the resistance feelings are out of harmony with the Bigger Picture?

II: Potentially. Sometimes a dissonance can increase your interest as it then later resolves into a more harmonious sound. Don't write-off resistance or dissonance as something to avoid – it has its purpose and can come in handy, especially for increasing appreciation through contrast.

Me: What do I do now that I've "listened," described all the parts of this exercise component, and seen the parts that are dissonant?

II: First off, appreciate the dissonance. Don't try to move out of it yet. See it as a contrast that is helping you refine your current vision.

Me: Yeah, as I look back at what I've said so far, I can see how my injured knee has helped me to re-evaluate which exercises will be the most sustainable and balanced lifestyle for me. It's probably not good for me to be 1000% gung-ho. And maybe that's also why I'm not *entirely* feeling inspired to have a yoga routine? Like that's too much stretching, and not enough aerobics, for what my body needs now?

II: That's entirely possible. More importantly, notice how you are already considering other possibilities for how to create your exercise component of your Ideal Body. When you embrace the dissonance, and allow yourself to feel it and appreciate it, it's a natural unfoldment to resolve toward more harmonious solutions.

Me: Yeah, like I feel inspired to look up some aerobic yoga routines to try those out – I usually only do gentle stretching types of yoga. And I'm also aware now that I've been holding a belief that I *need* to exercise in order to lose this weight – it's not possible for it to just fall off because of my mindset (no matter what that guided visualization says).

It's so crazy how I can shoot myself in the foot – trying to believe in a solution (like the statements in the guided visualization), while in a hidden corner of my mind I don't believe that solution is possible.

II: Yes, that's a pretty common occurrence in the human mind: thinking you're going for it, while still harboring doubts and disbelief.

Me: Geez, I can really feel the disharmony and dissonance with that! I'm saying one thing, but thinking another, so I'm not having an aligned harmony of thoughts.

II: Yes. And remember that it's OK to uncover, discover, explore, and experience dissonance. The contrasting sounds or experiences help you to refine your vision and align your actions for what you really want to create.

Me: So maybe I don't really want to be a runner or a yoga stretcher? I'm not really sure how to define myself as an exerciser.

II: That in itself is a great discovery. Rather than trying to define yourself by other people's models or societal expectations of what kind of exercise you *should* do, you have an opening in your mindspace now to explore and define your *own* vision of what it means to be an exerciser.

Me: OK, give me a sec…

THE INTENTION IDEA

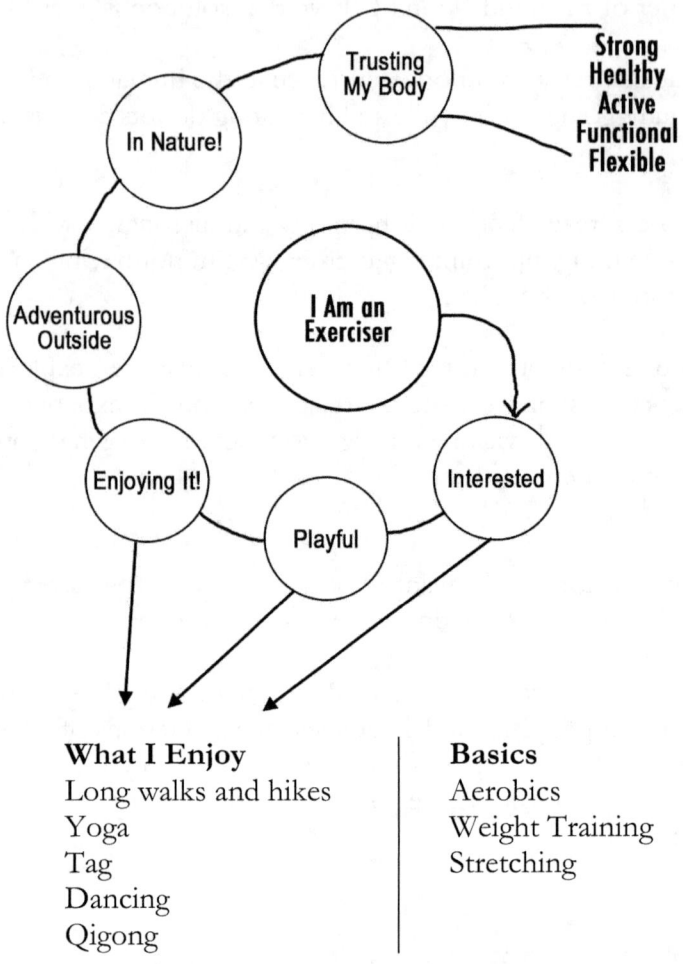

What I Enjoy	Basics
Long walks and hikes	Aerobics
Yoga	Weight Training
Tag	Stretching
Dancing	
Qigong	

Me: Interesting! When I mind map being an exerciser, I have no attention on losing weight and it's all about enjoying the use of my body in ways that are fun to me. If I try to incorporate "the basics" of what I think I should be doing, then I feel dissonance. But when I focus on doing what is enjoyable to my body (and my Spirit), I feel inspired to just do more of it.

I guess I'm still a little worried that doing what I enjoy won't be enough – that I'll be missing a key ingredient to exercise that everyone else knows you need to include in order to have a healthy body.

THE INTENTION IDEA

II: Actually, the key ingredient is *your* Vision, and your willingness to listen to and Follow Your Heart as you manifest your Vision. You'll notice that your Big Picture Vision has you healthy, functional, and strong ... pretty much all the things that the mind says you'll get if you follow its prescribed, socially-indoctrinated exercise plan. So, keep following your Vision and listen to how your Heart guides you to the perfect combination of solutions unique for you.

Me: Sounds good – worth trying out (I still don't trust it entirely).

II: It's OK to build Trust through experience. Clearly you have had experiences of doing what your mind thought was reasonable. Now try a different approach of Following your Heart to see how that works for you.

Me: I love it when you help me appease and coax my mind into following my heart. ☺

II: Whatever it takes to help you grow your skills at navigating life from a heart-centered, Universe-connected approach! ☺

Me: This seems like it was fairly easy to bring an area of my life back into harmony again. Is what I did really all there is to it? I mean, I pretty much just explored a component of my vision so I could feel what parts were in alignment and harmony, and what was feeling dissonant. Then I appreciated the dissonant parts, mostly by looking more closely at my vision for this area of my life, and clarifying what I really want to create for *my* unique vision. That, in itself, inspired me to try some new actions, attitudes, beliefs, and approaches more in alignment with my vision. Is that really all I've got to do in order to determine how to adjust, continue, or stop my actions and causes for the results I want to create?

II: Try it out on the exercise topic and report back. ☺

PART 4

APPLICATION

DAY 54

Me: Hey, I feel like we are nearing the end of our conversation about Following Your Heart (if our conversations ever really end). What do you think about moving into some focused dialogue about applying all the tools and ideas we've been discussing? I'm envisioning us having a few more spaces between conversations while I take actions toward my intentions. Maybe we could have more conversations that reflect on my personal study and use of these tools. What do you think?

II: Yes, I think that is an important and necessary component of our exploration together. Just as we have done, a few times, in using examples from your own life, it would be helpful and valuable to include some additional real-life examples and experience. This will further refine our exploration, and it will model how these tools and ideas can be flexibly molded and applied to unique situations and unique consciousnesses.

Me: What do you think about asking a few friends to play along and also share their unique experiences with you and these tools?

II: Absolutely! The more the merrier in this Universe! Let's all play together and create some new harmonies! ☺

Me: Do you have any suggested guidelines for me and my friends on how to work with you and these tools, and how to document our results for this next part of our exploration together?

II: You know my only suggested rule: Lighten Up! ☺

And for those minds that prefer more structure, here are a few ideas:
- Read through all our conversations and have a paper copy you can flip through – or at least a paper copy of the

intention-work easy reference guide.
- Pick an intention you want to focus on for your exploration of applying the tools.
- Start wherever you are with that intention. That may mean looking at the easy reference guide to feel where you're at. Or maybe hold the intention in your mind and intuitively turn to a page of the book for some part of our conversation to inspire you. Or ask me a question about your intention and feel or automatic-write my answer. In other words, engage with me and these ideas and tools, and start taking some kind of action – any kind.

As for documenting our exploration together and the results of how you mold the tools to your unique scenario, record whatever feels pertinent, sacred, and important to you in whatever mode feels the most alive and juicy to you. In the end, this is all about your enjoyable journey and however you prefer to create it, so I have absolutely no attachment to how you play with, or transform, these tools and ideas to meet your current needs and desires. Have fun exploring, creating, and spreading your intention-creating wings and taking flight with them. There are no limits, and the possibilities are endless!

DAY 55

Me: Apparently where I'm at on my journey of losing weight, and creating a body I love to live in, is in a phase of word play. So, according to the easy reference guide: phase two, Direction, writing intention statements. I've been writing down and trying on a few intention statements to see how they feel, what wordings resonate most, and just enjoying exploring what it is I really want to create. Here are a few of my current faves:

My body loves me.
I keep my body healthy and happy.
The older I get, the healthier I get.
I am an exerciser.
My body loves to move!

(I came up with that yesterday and it popped into my head a couple of times while walking and it felt really good!)

My body uses fat to fuel me.

This one feels a little weird, so I started exploring how I would like my body to use fat. That got me thinking about using resources in general, and storing resources (like storing fat on the body, hoarding stuff because I might need it someday, and saving money just in case). I compared that storing mentality with a sense of abundance and flow, and the idea that everything I need is always available to me. I like the idea of being in the Flow, so I came up with this series of intention statements:

Money moves through me.

(This gave me a visual of a torus energy field, where money comes in to me, flows out into the external environment to be used, and flows back in again.)

THE INTENTION IDEA

Food moves through my body.

(Feels like food is being used by all my cells exactly as it needs to, and the rest is expelled with ease.)

Ideas move through me.

(Feels like being a human manifesting and sharing ideas is a valuable contribution to the planet.)

I am a clear channel for Light.

(Feels like being a clear, quartz, crystal prism – light comes into me and is refracted out in many colors and perspectives based on my unique combination of beliefs, attitudes, and intentions.)

I take what I need and let go what I don't.

I have a little hesitation on saying "I take." I have some social indoctrinations that say I shouldn't take – I should receive what's offered, but not ask for more. And definitely don't take more than what's offered – that's greedy, or even stealing. But, when the phrase is used by someone offering advice, then it feels really good: Take what resonates and leave what doesn't. Hmmm…

I take what resonates and leave what doesn't.

That totally works for me now. I think I'll keep playing with both phrases for a bit to see what kinds of experiences they each create.

* * *

Ohh! I found an even better version for me of that last statement:

I take what resonates and let the rest Be.

For me, that has a lovely feel of letting things that don't resonate for me just be as they are. I don't need to make them wrong or push against them. They can continue to exist, and I might even

THE INTENTION IDEA

appreciate them for what they are, while I focus more of my attention on the things that do resonate with me now. That phrasing feels very spacious to me – like everything is all right.

DAY 56

Me: I can feel how the long hike analogy is so helpful for me while on the way to manifesting my intention. Once I have an idea of what I want to create, I often feel very impatient that I can't snap my fingers and just have it now.

For my weight loss and ideal body intention, I am eager to purge the extra weight in my tummy. It feels uncomfortable, like I'm bloated, and my clothes don't fit as well as they used to. Nevertheless, I held back this morning from "pushing the river" by taking more psyllium seed capsules. I felt an intuition to add more fiber, and specifically psyllium seed, to my daily routine to help clear out what feels like sludge and constipation from my digestion. I took one capsule and got some movement, so it was tempting to take a lot more. But the idea of a long hike popped into my awareness, and I thought my body would like a gentler approach of adding a little more fiber at a time, more gradually, rather than dumping it all in.

It feels a little weird not to put my foot down hard on the gas pedal when it seems like I've got something that's working toward manifesting my intention. But apparently this isn't a sprint to the finish line.

II: It rarely is a sprint to manifest an intention. And even when the Universe does move quickly, it still has a graceful, intuitive Flow to it. You will always be able to stay present and appreciative of what-is while you are creating your intentions. You never need to experience a "mad dash" or sense of "hurry." The more present you are with what-is, the more grace you will experience as you move through time and the physical realms – no matter what your pace.

DAY 57

Me: I found another way the long hike analogy helps me! I notice that my mind really wants to find "the one thing" or "the missing piece" – that if I just did *that* one thing, I'd get the results I want. When I think of my intention manifestation as a long hike, it seems much more natural and obvious that there will be several parts of the puzzle that need to be gathered, and put together, in order to achieve full manifestation. For example, I might add some bodyweight-based strength training into my exercise routine, since the idea crossed my path the other day and it felt like a potentially fun thing for me to explore. I'm going to add that to my regimen of increased fiber intake and all the walking and hiking I already do.

I guess I'm more aware of how valuable it is to take in, and try out, new actions and ideas on my intention-creation path. My friend was just telling me how she found a book about paleo eating and exercise she's going to follow to lose weight. I could feel how her mind had latched on to the hope of "a perfect solution" and some rules to follow that would "guarantee" success since it had worked well for the author of the book. I've been in that hopeful mindset before (and often), clinging to the idea that *this* panacea will give me what I want. But from a long-hike perspective, I see how my path is unique, and it's valuable for me to pick and choose the actions and ideas that feel like they'll serve me best in this moment, rather than blindly or hopefully following someone else's trail.

II: Well, it *is* OK to follow someone else's trail, just best if you do it with your eyes open, and with a willingness and attentiveness to adjusting your course as needed for your present circumstances.

Me: And OK to bring in other ideas besides what is prescribed?

II: With reason, yes. Some paths don't mix well with others, but *all* paths are open to change and to modification for present circumstances.

Me: How do I know if it's a path that blends well with others?

II: Follow your intuition – *always* follow your intuition. 🙏

DAY 58

Me: I found yet another aspect of the long hike analogy that's working really well for me. My mind is really good at planning and making to-do lists, but it's easy for me to feel a sense of urgency to get everything on my list done. When it comes to taking action toward my intention, I'm prone to feeling that same urgency. Kind of like, "hurry up and try and do everything in order to manifest the intention." But when I remember the hike analogy, the urgency relaxes a bit and it's easier to be in exploration mode.

For example, I've had several ideas of actions to take toward achieving my ideal body. Some I've done a little of already – a colon cleanse on the weekend, a few experiments with psyllium and fiber options, and a bit more walking during my day. On Saturday, I had the opportunity to dance for a couple of hours at an event, and I really enjoyed moving my body around to the music. Near the end of the event, someone came up to me and asked if I did ecstatic dance. I told her I hadn't been to an ecstatic dance in years, but I do like that freeform type of dance. Then I asked her what made her ask me if I did ecstatic dance – I mean, was I dancing in a certain way that says "ecstatic dancer"? She replied that she only asked because I'd been dancing for pretty much the whole event, so I must like to dance, and she thought I'd like ecstatic dance.

This totally felt like a nudge from the Universe to do more dance as exercise for my body. Especially since she then told me about a group of people who go regularly to an ecstatic dance event on Wednesday nights. I took the nudge and made plans to skip qigong class and go to the next Wednesday ecstatic dance to try it out again. But then, on Tuesday, I got an email that this week's qigong class would be a special, one-time class where we'd learn "qigong weight lifting."

At this point I could feel my mind conflicted about what to do. But from a hike analogy perspective it didn't feel like anything was going to be left undone — I was just detouring to look at some wildflowers before continuing on to the lake that was my next intended destination.

So, I went to qigong class and it was awesome! I learned a whole new way of weight lifting that I actually enjoy, and that incorporates the qigong energetics and confidence building. I love it. And next week I'll make it to the ecstatic dance event, which turns out to be perfectly timed because my qigong instructor happens to be going out of town and cancelling class next week.

Could it be more aligned and in the Flow, this exploration I'm on!?

II: Yes, it will keep getting better and better. 🙏

DAY 59

Me: Just under a month has passed since I last wrote, and I've continued to enjoy my exploration of creating my ideal body. I had a visit with my naturopath that put a lot of my journey in perspective. The last time I visited, a little over two months ago, I formed a vision of my ideal health: having exercise routines that can last me into older ages, my clothes fitting well, being active in my body, being able to run on a hiking trail if I want to, and feeling flexible and relaxed. It was at my last appointment that my doctor told me about *The Gabriel Method* and it was nice to be able to report back how much that guided visualization has helped. I definitely feel healthier and happier in my body, I am more calm and relaxed, and it seems my life is getting better and better and better (just like he says in the guided visualization). When weighed, I hadn't lost any weight, but because I feel good about my body and my path of exploration, it didn't bother me as much that *that* particular measurement of my ideal body had not changed yet. I also have a potential new puzzle piece to play with in the form of a homeopathic liver detox my doctor has me using for the next two months. I feel strangely relaxed, happy, and on track for manifesting my intention, even though I don't have a *lot* of physical evidence of progress yet. It feels like all my progress is mental and emotional so far. Although I will say that's a huge win to still have a positive attitude, and motivation to keep going, even without physical evidence of success or all the results I want.

II: Yes, it's good that you are focusing your attention on the parts of your intention that *are* manifesting, and not over-dramatizing the lack of results in the parts of your intention that are still in process. It's *so* all about your delightful journey. Don't get sidetracked trying to leap to the end results when there is so much to experience and explore along the way.

DAY 60

Me: I just re-read our day 52 conversation about driving vs. relaxing, and letting go my measurements and evaluations. I intentionally re-read it because I notice I'm still having some doubts about whether I'm being too relaxed about creating my intentions – too "go with the flow." I can tell I have some limiting beliefs about letting things be easy, having it be this good, and deserving it to be this good and easy. It feels like I've put a constraint on a hose so that I don't get too much goodness flowing in on me at once. In fact, now that I think about it, I do feel a little worried about what might happen if I have it too good. I don't have specific scenarios in mind, but I do feel a sense of concern – like "waiting for the other shoe to drop." Got any suggestions on how to explore and handle this?

II: It's good you re-read that section. I'm going to remind you again of what I said there:

"From a Universal Energy perspective, you never need to push."

It seems you need some further clarification on how the Universal Evolution works without pushing.

Me: Yes, please!

II: The Universe has a natural momentum of evolution. There's no stopping it now. No matter how much you might slow down, or even feel stagnant at times, the Universe continues to evolve. Even if *many* of you humans slow down or appear stagnant, the Universe's evolution continues.

Consider the life of a butterfly as an example. The caterpillar appears to be very busy eating and growing into a bigger and bigger caterpillar. And then, at some point, it feels called to find a place to to build a cocoon and be still. Through that outer stillness, and inner changes, it transforms into a butterfly.

There is no doubt that all of your inspired actions, and inspired stillness, are leading you forward in your own evolution.

Me: But how do I make sure my actions or stillness are inspired and not done out of reaction or selfishness?

II: Pay attention to your question from a feeling place instead of a worried mind state. What does it feel like when you are inspired?

Me: It feels energizing, happy, delicious. It has a kind of sense of "rightness" to it – like this is where I'm supposed to be. But that rightness feeling is still open and listening. It doesn't feel like I've locked in the answer. It feels like I'm following a trail, or a scent, or some kind of sensation that is leading me in a certain direction, moment-by-moment, without seeing very far ahead where this trail is going.

II: Yes – that's a good description of listening to your Higher Self and following your intuition.

Now, what does it feel like when you are acting, or still, out of reaction or selfishness?

Me: It feels like being a little kid throwing a temper tantrum or refusing to do something because I really don't want to. It also feels forceful – like taking something because I want it, and not considering anyone else in the process.

Maybe that's my concern – it's just *so* easy to be focused on myself and what *I* want, that it feels challenging to make sure I'm still connecting with others and considering the greater good in all that I'm doing.

II: Nobody said you need to think about the greater good all the time. But just notice how mental, judgmental, and doubtful you became as soon as you tapped in to the feelings of reaction and selfishness?

Me: Yes, I definitely went there.

II: So how about you keep a practice for a few days of discerning how you feel? If you feel mental, judgmental, or doubtful, then deliberately tune in to your Higher Self, and feel for your Inspired Next Step.

Me: And if I'm feeling energized, happy, and delicious from following my Higher Self, how do I allow all of that good to come rushing in without limiting it?

II: You're right, there are some limiting beliefs there blocking you from taking it all in. Let's explore more of that tomorrow. For now, follow your intuition. ☺

DAY 61

Me: I've been tuning in to my Higher Self more and more, wherever and whenever I can think of it. I got a phrase from the Wayne Dyer book I've been reading that especially helps when I'm feeling judgmental or separate from others:

> "The same life force that flows through me, flows through you."

I really like how that thought helps me to feel the sacredness and connectedness of all life, while still appreciating each of our unique differences. I've also been playing with the thought:

> "It's OK to enjoy all this."

I still feel a little resistance – like a worry that I'm slacking off. But I also feel a bit more appreciation, gratitude, and presence with what-is.

What else can I do to explore and release any limitations I have on letting all the good in?

II: Your exploration of thoughts – some new ways of looking at things – is a very good place to start. Your qigong instructor often expresses a thought worthy of your consideration:

> "Accessing High level energies, with no limitations – infinite potential."

In fact, that phrase "infinite potential" is a good mantra for you to roll around in your consciousness for a while. It has the feel of the ever-expanding Universe.

Me: Yes, that does feel good. But how do I open to all the good I am receiving and experiencing?

II: It does seem like you put up some quick walls of "I don't deserve this," "it can't be this good – there must be something I'm missing," and "there must be something wrong with it." Mostly it feels like a core idea of "it can't be this good."

Me: Yes, that resonates. It feels like I'll get in trouble, or have some kind of negative consequence, if things are working out well for me. Thus, I often have the feeling of waiting for the other shoe to drop. Heck, it's probably so ingrained that *I* will drop another shoe – I will find or create some kind of negative consequence just to balance out all the good that is flowing in. I really feel a bit suspicious if it's "too good."

II: Sounds like you've discovered a rock (obstacle) on your path to work around.

Me: So, use the Rock Questions? I'm afraid that will be too simple and easy. (I'm *almost* laughing at myself, except that I'm still tangled up in this limitation).

II: You'll be laughing and smiling soon enough. Start with the Rock Questions.

Me: OK.
1. What's really going on here?
I feel worried that I'll have it "too good" and will have some kind of negative consequence for having it so good. It's such a strong belief that I will knowingly (or unknowingly) create a negative consequence. Or I'll just re-direct my attention to a problem, rather than allowing myself to experience the infinite potential of the goodness.

2. Why is it important?
I want to resolve it so I can keep evolving with the infinite potential for goodness. I might have put the limit there as a way of staying connected with people who aren't experiencing all the goodness – or

in case they have judgments of people who are experiencing all the goodness. I can definitely see times in my childhood when I had a *lot* of goodness flowing my way, and I felt I had to protect myself from appearing or becoming "spoiled" from having so much good come my way with so little effort.

3. What are the feelings and sensations involved?
Feels like guilty pleasure – enjoying something I'm not meant to have because I didn't *earn* it (by working hard to create it).

4. What are the thoughts, ideas, and beliefs, especially the ones on repeating loops, around this topic?
I don't deserve it. This is *too* good. Can it really be this good? It probably won't last. People won't like me. Who do you think you are? That's just *too* special. You have to be careful not to get spoiled.

Wow, especially that last one. I hadn't realized how very much attention I have put on being *careful* not to get spoiled – my whole life. I didn't want to *be* a spoiled brat, or be *judged* or labeled as a spoiled brat by others. Ironically, since I can't control how others choose to label me, I've been trying to avoid that label by creating negative consequences for myself whenever anything starts to get "too good" by my estimation.

Well that exploration makes the obstacle more visible and manageable now. I'm going to take a little time to explore and imagine some alternatives to this idea of being "spoiled."

II: Sounds like a good direction! Let me know what you uncover. 🙏

DAY 62

Me: I was exploring synonyms of the word "spoiled" and found some interesting distinctions in my consciousness.

To me, spoiled has a connotation of not deserving the goodness, or not respecting what was received. The "not deserving" part seems to show up as a feeling that I have to do something (like work hard) in order to earn the goodness. The "treating the goodness with respect" aspect feels like an obligation to seriously recognize how lucky I am, and do something to pay it forward.

I can see how I adopted these viewpoints when I was growing up in an upper-middle-class family. My parents put a lot of attention on making sure I valued all the benefits and goodness they gave me, without becoming a spoiled brat. I also was aware of a sense of separation from my friends, who didn't have all the types of goodness I had, and wanting to minimize my specialness to avoid jealousies or a feeling of disconnection.

But knowing where this came from isn't nearly as helpful as finding a new path and label that works better for me, for where I am now. As I explored synonyms of the word spoiled, I landed on the word Blessed.

When I consider feeling Blessed, it doesn't have any upper limits to it, no need to do anything to deserve it, and no *need* to pay it forward. It feels like full-on enjoyment and appreciation of all the good that is in my life right now.

For me, Blessed has a sense of blessings being bestowed on me from God, or the Universe. It feels like an unquestionable authority is giving me the blessing, so it is undeniable that I deserve it. Also, since I perceive blessings as a gift from God, it's more obvious that I can, should, and will enjoy it. It feels like "my cup runneth over," so any "paying it forward" is a natural expression of my enjoyment and doesn't need to be planned or forced from a place of obligation.

Now here's where I'm laughing at the whole creation: for the past year I've been driving around with a sign in my car that says:

> I Am So Blessed!

A friend gave it to me and I've been enjoying looking at it consciously. Apparently, it's been working its way into my subconscious too. ☺

II: Yes, and now you are ready to deliberately own your Blessed creation from the perspective of your super-conscious – as a Higher Self deciding how to create your forward experiences. Nice work and exploration!

Me: Thanks! I feel very Blessed! ☺

DAY 63

Me: I'm not sure where I'm at in the phases of intention-work, but something has been on my mind I'd like your perspectives on.

For the last two weeks, I've been working at a faster pace than usual to get some projects done at work that had tight timelines and hard due dates. The contrast of that time-based schedule, compared to the rest of my "lazy days of summer" experience I've been creating, got me thinking about the concept of pressure.

I know I've received a lot of indoctrinations about how to create with pressure. Time pressure to get things done, peer pressure to be a certain way, and pressure to perform well. Even using an accountability partner feels like an attempt to use pressure to motivate me to create a certain result within a certain time frame.

While creating with pressure works – I mean look at diamonds made out of coal – I feel like our intention-work is opening doors to some additional ways of creating. More of a creating-with-the-Flow approach than creating under pressure.

I asked Dan his perspectives on what it takes to create with the Flow and this is what we came up with together:
1. Listen to what's really happening and what's really needed now.
2. Follow your intuition. If you feel resistance, handle it. If you don't, then look for right-timing.
3. Be open to things manifesting different than you planned.
4. Hold the Bigger Picture Intention, and feel for how to create toward that now. Accept any answer you get.
5. You know you're creating with the Flow when you feel a sense of Oneness with the Universe – like you are a channel, or vehicle, for the Universe to express through you. Or, you lose that clinging sense of "mine" and you feel more connected to everyone and everything.

Maybe I'm exploring some aspects of the Experience and Evolution phase, as my intentions expand out into new intention waves? But I don't feel finished with any of my intentions yet. What are your perspectives on this topic?

II: As usual, you have a lot of thoughts. ☺ It's good you are exploring these indoctrinated aspects of creating. Pulling apart the default responses helps you to re-examine them and choose more deliberately how you would like to structure your creations.

So yes, creating with the Flow is much more aligned with intention-work than creating under pressure. That's not to say that you can't still manifest your intentions while under pressure. It's just that pressure adds another variable into your mind-space that can muddy your intention waters.

Me: Why does pressure muddy my intention waters?

II: For most humans, pressure comes with a lot of judgments and resistances. You judge yourself for performing well, or poorly, under pressure. Perhaps you resist any disapproval, or other consequences, if you don't fulfill the desired outcomes within the pressure framework. As you noticed, pressure isn't bad. It is used to turn coal into diamonds and to relax tense muscles in a massage. It's really your judgments, and resistances to outcomes, that can cause complications when you introduce pressure into your intention-work.

Me: So, try not to use pressure in intention-work?

II: More like, work on releasing your judgments and resistances so that you *can* use it if you need or want to.

Me: How do I do that?

II: The Rock Questions? ☺ It's always a good place for you to start, to better understand how your unique consciousness has built structures around this topic.

Me: OK, I'll do that next. And what about what phase of intention-work I'm in? Does it matter if I know or don't know where I'm at?

II: Of course not. The phases are there to help you organize these concepts and have a Big Picture feel of how you can work to manifest your intentions. There are millions upon millions of ways intentions can manifest, just as there are millions upon millions of humans manifesting millions upon millions of intentions. Remember, I offer you guidelines and perspectives, not rules. ☺

DAY 64

Me: On to the Rock Questions about pressure ...
1. What's really going on here?
When I feel any kind of pressure to create (time, performance, needed results) I get more tense and intense about the creation. I think I even lose sight of the Bigger Picture intention, because I'm so focused on trying to control the minute details in order to get a specific outcome.

I don't feel relaxed or in the Flow, and it's more likely I'll encounter obstacles. Or at least, it's more obvious when I do encounter obstacles, because my immediate response is frustration.

I feel like I learned to create under pressure in school with deadlines, grades, and a lot of approval and disapproval from peers and authority figures.

When I think of pressure, I feel constrained and the "push the river" type of consciousness. There's a lot of "should, have to, need to, must do" kinds of thoughts. I don't feel connected to the Universe and Bigger Picture. Instead, it feels like a very normal, mundane human experience.

2. Why is it important?
There are going to be times when I want to create within a timeline, meet a deadline, or I need to achieve a certain outcome. I'd like to be able to do that without getting all tensed up and mental. It seems like there ought to be a way to stay in my Heart-space, and create with the Flow, even when there is a time pressure or "required" outcome.

3. What are the feelings and sensations involved?
Tenseness. Feels like I'll be judged for coloring outside the lines, instead of having my artwork appreciated just the way it is. Feels like I *need* a perfect outcome – or else.

My neck and shoulders especially get very tense and it feels like my mind goes into overdrive.

4. What are the thoughts, ideas, and beliefs, especially the ones on repeating loops, around this topic?
"Have to …." That repeats a lot. "It won't be OK," or "I won't be OK if …."

Memories of times I missed the deadline, or wasn't performing well enough for someone, and the lasting disappointment, shame, and guilt for not doing better. Feels like those specific events are evidence that my best isn't good enough.

Just the other day, I told that intention to a friend: "My Best Is Good Enough." She immediately asked, "How do you know if your best is good enough?" It feels like it is, because it's all I've got. But what about all those times I was pushed or pressured to go farther than I thought I could, and it came out even better? How do I know if I've really given my best? How do I judge or decide what is good enough on a project without it becoming all-consuming and taking time away from other projects and life activities?

It feels like there's an underlying belief that I can't know what's best.

Wow. Just feeling into that belief, I can see how it keeps me from ever being truly satisfied with my work, or for that matter, being *confident* in what I've done. I'll always be wondering if I should have done something more – as long as I have that belief.

I'm going to big-H Handle[5] it right now and see what opens up! ☺

Oh, I just realized the full belief is "I can't know what's best, but other people can."

No wonder I have been tensing up under pressure – I would *never* feel good enough unless someone else tells me "it's OK, it's good

---

[5] Shout out to my friend G who once called our Avatar tools for removing and integrating unhelpful creations as "big-H Handling it."

enough." Whew! Glad I found that one! Now I'm excited to see what shifts in my experiences of creating with pressure.

DAY 65

Me: It's been just a couple of days since I found and big-H Handled that belief "I can't know what's best, but other people can." I can definitely feel a difference. It seems like I am more naturally treating "pressures" like a game or a fun challenge. For example, I say to myself, "I wonder if I can get that project done before it's time to leave today?"

It feels more fun to "race the clock," or work quickly and intently, and it doesn't feel like a disappointment if I don't meet my self-imposed challenge. I guess my answer to "how do you know if your best is good enough?" is "because I went for it!"

I feel a lot more Flow now too – like there's a lot more things working out with perfect timing, better than I had planned in my mind. And I feel happy! ☺

II: Yes, it's amazing how freeing yourself up from a rock (obstacle) in your mind can release so much more creative, Universal Power into your experience. As much as it is important to have an intention – and Go For It! – it's equally as important to find and remove any obstacles you encounter along the way.

Manifesting Intentions is an ongoing dance of creating what you prefer and Handling what you have resistance on. It's a delightful exploration, evolution, and unfolding of the Universe within your human experience.

Me: The way you talk about it makes it feel so very magical!

II: It is! ☺

DAY 66

Me: I had a new insight about manifesting my intentions that was inspired by my camping trip last weekend. We pitched our tent off of a forest service road, next to a stream. I could hear the stream bubbling, gurgling, and flowing along from everywhere at our camp site, including while inside our tent! I went to bed to the sound of a river flowing and woke up to the sound of a river flowing. It struck me as profound that the river is flowing 24 hours a day, 7 days a week – all the time!

It then occurred to me that life is always flowing too, and maybe instead of focusing my attention on arriving at some destination or endpoint where my intentions are finally manifested, I could instead focus on experiencing this never-ending flow of life.

I'm not entirely sure what this looks like, but I can feel how the shift of focus relaxes something inside of me. I don't feel an urgent pressure to prove myself or show that my intention has manifested. Especially when I think about my intention to have my ideal, healthy body – if I think of it as an endpoint destination, then I see I'm not all the way there yet, because I don't appear to have lost much weight. But when I look at my intention for my ideal, healthy body as if it were a constantly flowing river, then I feel like I'm right on track and all is well. I currently feel good in my body. I'm exercising in ways I like (hiking and qigong), I'm eating foods that feel nurturing, and I am following the paths of opportunity as they present themselves to me. For example, I'm currently focusing more attention on creating relaxed muscles by stretching more and changing my ergonomic setup at work. I don't know if I'll ever announce "mission achieved" with this intention, since it really is an intention to have my ideal, healthy body for the rest of my life, and my body's needs are often changing.

Come to think of it, my previous intention to have the perfect life partner for me was in some ways "checked off" 13 years ago because

I have Dan in my life, but I feel the intention is still flowing through my life, only now with the words "we are an aligned team." This relationship intention doesn't have a lot of my direct focus like it did when I was searching for my partner, but I can feel the intention is there, always flowing paths of opportunity for us to play, co-create, and love together.

What's your perspective on intentions that have a never-ending flow like this vs. ones that have a "mission achieved" endpoint to them?

II: You have stumbled across a Universal Truth in your flowing river experience:

>Nothing ever ends.

Sometimes things transform, and from a human viewpoint that transition from one state of being-ness to another feels like an ending and a new beginning. But from a Universal Energy perspective, the energy is continuing to flow, just sometimes on a different course or path.

As for intentions with endpoint destinations, even these "milestones" are part of the Bigger Picture evolution. Every part of the intention manifestation experience fuels forward growth for whatever is next in your Flow.

So yes, it's great that you are relaxing your attention that was super-focused on achieving goals, and that you are more deliberately enjoying the overall Flow of Life. Now you can have greater access to both modes of intention-creating: a continual flowing intention and a milestone intention (that will feed future intentions when it appears to be "done").

Me: Cool. So just keep going and enjoying life and all my intentions in all their many forms?

II: Exactly! Ride on!

DAY 67

Me: Feeling inspired from yesterday's conversation, I thought I'd write out my Flowing River Intentions (that I am holding life-long) vs. my Milestone Intentions (that I am focusing on manifesting in the near-term).

My Flowing River Intentions:
I have the perfect income sources for me.
Money moves through me.
My income keeps increasing.
Everyone wins!
We are an aligned team.
I keep my body healthy and happy.
I am an exerciser.
My life is aligned with service to Humanity.
I manifest delightful surprises.
I am living the life of my dreams!

My Current Milestone Intentions:
I create 300K/month in Ecom revenue at work.
I help bring Intention Idea to the World.
I pay off all my debts.

What I notice from writing these out, is that the Flowing River Intentions feel very open, relaxing, and spacious to me. It's like they are decisions about how I am orienting my attention and living my life – or like an expression of me.

The Milestone Intentions feel more constrained – like there's a time pressure or specific outcome to achieve. I feel like I'm more prone to measure and judge my progress toward manifesting these outcomes, and that gets me more in a mental state. I feel like I want to hurry up and manifest these intentions just to have the sweet relief of being done.

THE INTENTION IDEA

How can I relax or enjoy this pressure more, so that I don't get so mental and anxious about these milestone intentions?

II: *Enjoying* the pressure is a great perspective to take here. Relaxing the pressure on milestone intentions can lose some of your directional power – you can get so relaxed that you let the intention go and stop focusing attention on it. In contrast, *enjoying* the pressure can turn it more into a game or challenge. You can decide which intention(s) you want to focus on most, at any given time, and challenge yourself to see how far you can move the intention forward. And then enjoy it when you relax your attention from one intention and put it on another.

Also, it seems you still have some rocks (obstacles) on your path about judgments and measurements. Why don't you take a closer look at that?

Me: Will do!

DAY 68

Me: It's time to use the Rock Questions to explore what's in my way regarding pressure, judgments, and measurements.

1. What's really going on here?
When I set a specific goal, I feel pressure to make it happen and relief when it's done. It's like, while the intention is in process, I label myself as "not there yet," or "inferior," or "not good enough to make it." And then when my intention *is* realized, I label myself as a "winner," or "a huge success," or as "capable." I'm definitely happier with that second set of labels, and very uncomfortable with the labels I'm using while the intention is in process.

2. Why is it important?
I want to enjoy creating my milestone intentions as much as I enjoy the feel of my flowing river intentions. And I'd like to be kinder to myself with the labels I am automatically putting on myself and my progress.

3. What are the feelings and sensations involved?
Constraint, worry, concern about how I will be perceived by others, and doubt that I will ever complete my goal.

4. What are the thoughts, ideas, and beliefs, especially the ones on repeating loops, around this topic?
"I'm not good enough" immediately comes to mind, but I think it's playing softly in the background as a subliminal message. At least, if I were more consciously aware of it, I think I would notice it, turn it off, and choose a different thought.

"If I don't do it (complete the intention), then I'm a complete failure."

That one hits me like a sucker punch to the stomach. I wonder how many times I haven't gone for a milestone intention just to avoid

THE INTENTION IDEA

feeling like a failure? Or labeling myself as a failure?

"Once you start something you have to finish it."

"If you don't finish it, you're a quitter or you've given up."

"You can't know when it's OK to change directions or stop pursuing a goal – only someone else can decide that for you."

That one feels a lot like the belief I found the other day that "you can't know what's best, but other people can." This version feels more like I can't be trusted to steer my life with my own decisions – that I need an outside monitor to check on me and keep me on track.

In fact, as I think about that, I can remember all the times my mom and I talked about how valuable it was to have someone as a check and balance on our thoughts – to make sure we didn't get off track with too much ego or too much attachment to a preferred idea.

Huh! I see now, how much easier it is to trust my decisions when I am always open and considering other perspectives. But those other perspectives don't always have to come from outside of me. I can decide to explore many perspectives just by looking at things differently.

I do like sharing my perspectives with people I trust. I especially enjoy sharing with the people in the Avatar network, who I *know* have the skills to listen objectively and with appreciation – and without selfish or hidden motives.

Maybe that's the distinction I need to integrate and update my consciousness with now:

I can know when I'm attached to a decision, and need to consider alternative perspectives, vs. when I have openly considered many perspectives and landed on a direction for the present moment.

I'm going to take a little time for that to sink in.

DAY 69

Me: Re-reading my Rock Questions, I feel like an attitude that would help me while I'm in-process on a milestone intention is:

> I am capable.

I like the feel of that reminder: that even though I haven't manifested my intention yet, I am capable of navigating the long hike and taking whatever next steps are needed in order to keep that intention wave moving until it hits the shore.

I feel like my willingness to explore perspectives is part of what makes me capable to make that long hike. I also have to be able to decide which path of opportunity to follow next, based on what I've explored and what resonates for me.

Hmm, I'm starting to feel a little opening for enjoyment of my milestone intentions – like the idea *"this is going to be fun!"*

I'm going to keep rolling with that. ☺

II: Yes, roll on with these attitudes! When you expect it to be fun, and you expect that you are capable of meeting whatever challenges come your way, then you are in a state of adventure. And when you are adventuring, even pressure is a fun part of the journey. Enjoy the ride!

DAY 70

Me: I spent the weekend with friends who practice Hindu mantras and I was really moved by how profoundly I felt the intention in the mantras, even though they are in Sanskrit and I don't know exactly what's being said.

My friend told me that one of the mantras was about aligning my mind and actions with the "One Mind." When my friend was invoking that mantra, it felt like there was a deep current of intention – like a strong river – that we were aligning with. It felt like we were stepping into the flow of this intention by saying or tuning in to the mantra.

The experience made me realize how valuable it can be to align with an existing intention that has millions of humans repeating it and thousands of years of practice. It's like, instead of creating a new wave of intention with just my own thoughts, I'm tapping into the direction and power of a wave that has *many* people focused on it and putting their power behind it.

This brought up a couple more questions for me: How do I find more of these powerful intentions that already have *so* much energy in them, and are going in directions I also want to go?

If I have an intention that I've come up with myself, how do I make it as powerful as one of these long-time, big intention waves? Or how do I align my intention with one that already has a strong momentum?

What do you see as the difference between a personal intention and one of these "communal" intentions? How do I use both?

II: Let's start with your last question first. Because, yes, there is a distinction between an "individual" intention and a "communal" intention, and it's good for you to be aware of the differences and how to work with both.

In our time together we've been much more focused on the "individual" intentions, because these intentions are immediately accessible and created by you with all the resources you have within you right now. As you work more and more with your individual intentions, your senses about how your intention wants to flow and manifest will grow – and also your sense of when you need to give your intention another energetic push of creating power.

"Communal" intentions are just as you have described it: millions (or lots) of people over thousands (or many) years, that same intention has been held, given energy to, kept as sacred, and acted upon. When you align your thoughts and intentions with a communal intention, it takes less "push" from you and your energy to manifest the intention. What is required is your full alignment with the intention that is already in motion and already manifesting in the Universe. Most often a communal intention will be for a Big Picture goal or manifestation, like World Peace, Human Awakening, Alignment with Higher Vibration Consciousness, and Acting in Harmony, Appreciation, and Equanimity with the Universe.

A communal intention could be used for a group project – like raising a barn, building a community with a defined set of values, or achieving a common goal. However, this type of communal intention is usually shorter-term and ends when the project is completed, or when the participants in the intention let their attention drift and move on to other intentions. This happens a lot in the world of Intentions, so when you find a communal intention toward a Big Picture goal that doesn't really have an end point, and has been sustained sacredly for many years by many people, you can't help but feel the depth of Power and strong current of energy in that Intention wave.

Me: That makes me think of the qigong lineage I tap into when I practice my qigong movements and meditations.

II: Yes, exactly! There is so much support, power, healing energy, manifesting power, and directed Flow when you tap into the sacred practices of a lineage that has so very much human intention poured into it, *and* it is still alive – still practiced by humans today.

Me: So how do I find these types of Big Picture, Sacred, Communal Intentions?

II: One of the keys is to look for what is being held as sacred and practiced with reverence.

Me: How do I do that? How do I know if something is being practiced with reverence?

II: You can feel it. When something is treated as sacred, it is treated with respect and guarded against defamation. If you approach every person and every ritual or action as sacred, valuable, and important, then you are more likely to be allowed to see the full power and value in the person, ritual, or action.

Most people treat new ideas, ways of doing things, and even other people with some level of suspicion, disregard, discontent, or any flavor of judgment that conveys disrespect instead of honor and consecration. These attitudes and frames of mind prevent you from seeing and exploring *all* of the sacred and powerful communal intentions that are currently in motion. But if you stay open, respectful, and honoring of everyone you meet and every action and idea you see, then you have more chance of discovering new Communal Intentions.

Me: Are Communal Intentions usually associated with a religion or a defined social group?

II: They often are, but they don't have to be. And just because a sacred ritual is practiced by a large group of people over many years, that doesn't always make it powerful *or* beneficial.

THE INTENTION IDEA

The energy given to the Communal Intention, by each individual contributing to the intention with their thoughts and actions, determines its current power.

And whether the Communal Intention is beneficial to you is something you have to decide based on where you are wanting to go in your life – what you want to experience.

Me: How do I find the communal intentions that are going in directions I also want to go?

II: Start by holding your personal, individual intentions and keep exploring what the Bigger Picture of your intentions leads toward.

For example, you might first be focused on an intention to bring in more income to your personal finances and to have work that is enjoyable to you. As you experience manifesting that personal intention, you may discover that while you receive more money and enjoyable work, you are also able to enjoy giving people around you more harmonious and stress-free work lives. As you tune in to this aspect of creating more harmony and less stress for everyone, you might notice that you keep having opportunities to help people grow and stretch into new skill sets and responsibilities.

Now step back from this experience a little more – widen back your view from the specifics – and see a pattern of helping humanity to evolve by appreciating what-is while also stretching to experience more.

Do you see and feel that?

Me: Yes, I do. I feel like you just summed up the last five years of my life – or maybe more. ☺

II: Yes, it's a grand theme for you, that you are carving with every action in your life.

THE INTENTION IDEA

So now tune in further to this intention to help humanity evolve. Where else do you see, feel, or experience that intention?

Me: Lots of places. The Avatar network, the mantras my friend was saying last weekend, a lot of my friends who do various kinds of energy healing work, all the different personal development groups I've explored ….

II: Exactly! Now choose to see *all* of these human endeavors as one movement toward helping humanity evolve. How does that feel?

Me: Big. Really Big. It feels like a large river with a strong current or momentum that can't be stopped as it rushes toward the ocean. No matter what form the human evolution takes, there's no stopping it or changing its direction. We are going to evolve, no matter what.

II: That is the Communal Intention you are feeling and tapping into. And that's a great example of how you can find it: start with your individual intentions, feel for the Bigger Picture they feed into, sense the pattern or theme of the overall Intention, see how *all* of the individual intentions align with the Bigger Picture, and you are now in the Flow of the Communal Intention!

Me: Wow.

Now that I can see and feel the communal intention that my individual intentions align with, what do I do?

II: Ride the Wave. Keep your attention focused both on your individual intention that is your current personal expression of the Bigger Picture Intention, *and* keep some attention focused on the Bigger Picture Intention so that your actions stay aligned with the larger wave of momentum.

When you keep some attention on the Bigger Picture, Communal Intention, you will find it easier to keep sanctifying your intentions –

holding them as sacred.

When you treat your intentions with the same respect, care, and gratitude as anything else you hold sacred, you are adding power to their manifestation momentum.

Me: How can I treat your manifestation with even more respect, care, gratitude, and sanctity?

II: I feel you do quite a bit by honoring how I choose to come into form in the world, and not pushing the river to try to make something happen that your mind thinks is best.

So, keep honoring my voice, my flow.

Continuing to tune in to my energetic vibration also keeps my manifestation a sacred process. If you tune out, drop, or ignore an intention, it's like saying you don't care anymore.

That doesn't mean you need to be on a strict schedule of tuning in, or doing a daily ritual of connecting to your intentions. But ideally, you are so "in Love" with your intentions that you enjoy connecting with them, tuning in to their current flow, and "asking how they are doing" as it were.

Me: So, how are you doing?

II: Good! I've enjoyed the expansiveness of this exploration of Communal Intentions and I can feel we have some good, new explorations coming up.

DAY 71

Me: Last night Dan and I went to a presentation about EMF (electro-magnetic field) protections, and the speaker talked about how our heart is a magnetic field generator. He said many qigong and other masters have used amplification of the heart field as a form of protection against EMF and any other toxic substances or vibrations that would be detrimental to the body, mind, or spirit.

I was struck by this part of the presentation, because I was expecting him to say that the mind creates a magnetic field, since our thoughts have the power to attract (or repel) experiences. I feel like I'm back at square one in our exploration of mind-stuff vs. heart approaches. I'd love to hear your current perspectives on how the Heart-space works as a magnetic field generator – especially with respect to how to leverage that magnetic field for manifesting intentions.

II: I believe what caught your attention is actually a nuance of how the heart and mind work together. Without a mind, you would not be able to form the thoughts and ideas that go with the Heart-space feeling of your intention. So really, they work seamlessly together to create the magnetic field that attracts and repels.

Me: Does it help to focus more on one or the other while I'm creating my intentions? I mean, once I have the words of my intention, it's easy for me to hang out in mind-space, trying to figure out and achieve my next steps toward my goal. Should I be doing more heart-based work, like the heart breathing the speaker introduced us to last night?

II: You know my answer: There are no rules. 🖐

If you feel inclined to focus more on your heart-space than your mind-space, it's perfectly fine and great for you to practice the heart breathing, or any other techniques that you enjoy for focusing your

THE INTENTION IDEA

attention on your heart-space.

The key to creating your intentions is to keep creating balance in your approach. If you use your mind a lot, also use your heart. If you use your heart a lot, also use your mind.

You humans are more powerful creators than you usually realize, so an ongoing, continued exploration of what works for you in the present moment will always reveal a new aspect of intention-work that can open new doors of possibility for you.

So yes, go ahead and explore the heart breathing, and notice what the focus on your heart's magnetic field does for you.

Me: OK, I'll report back soon! ☺

Heart Breathing
(as described by Chaz Pro)
Focus attention on your heart-space.
Breathe in through your heart.
Breathe out through your heart.

You can also visualize watermelon pink and green colors in your heart-space.

DAY 72

Me: I've been doing the heart breathing technique and focusing on my heart-space for a few days now. I'm not sure what to report back about it yet.

Focusing my attention on my heart-space feels a little like the qigong practice of putting light attention on my dan tien (the energy center just below the navel). But it's also different. When I put attention on my dan tien, I have a sense of this pool of energy that is slowly growing in intensity and size.

When I put attention on breathing in and out of my heart-space, I have a sense of connecting with the Universal Flow of energy. It's like I'm breathing in energy from the Universe and recirculating it back out to the Universe through the torus of my heart field.

As my qigong instructor says, "the sensations you may or may not get while practicing are not so important as the intention you are holding." I feel like I need to add an intention to this heart breathing. The sensations are clear for me, but I'm not sure where I'm going with it.

II: Yes, it is a practice that has a lot of room for you to add intentions to it. Heart Breathing, in and of itself, helps you be aware of your Heart-Space and your connectedness to the Flow of the Universe. You get to have an experience in your body of how you draw energy from the Universe and give energy to the Universe.

Perhaps you could contemplate what you would like to draw in and give back with these Heart Breaths?

Me: Yes, I like that direction of focus. I feel like a lot of times my intentions are overly focused on what I want to receive, and it would be nice to pair that with what I am giving as a result of that receiving.

As an example, I would like to receive a new housemate to rent the extra bedroom and share space with Dan and I. What I am giving as a result of that receiving is a friendly, community vibration that shares resources and is helpful.

Mmmm, I'm going to walk and heart-breathe with that for a little bit....

DAY 73

Me: Wow! I'm really loving the effects of this Heart Breathing *with* an intention.

When I took my walk and breathed in my intention of having a new housemate, and breathed out the contribution of helping a fellow human being, I felt a deep peace about the intention.

That inspired me to explore the in-and-out heart breath, the receiving and giving, of *all* my milestone intentions. And of course, once I got started, I wanted to explore this "full-circle with the Universe" aspect for my flowing river intentions too. Here's how it came out during my exploration:

Milestone Intentions
In: I create 300K/month in Ecom Revenue.
Out: Success for *everyone*.

In: I help bring Intention Idea to the world.
Out: Clarity, Curiosity, and Harmony.

In: I pay off all my debts.
Out: I can help more people.

Flowing River Intentions
In: I am an exerciser.
Out: My body loves me and we are an aligned team.

In: I am living the life of my dreams!
Out: Gratitude (for *everything!*)

In: I manifest delightful surprises.
Out: Magic is everywhere! 🙏

THE INTENTION IDEA

In: I have the perfect income sources for me.
Out: I am on the right track. Peace. Everything is all right.

In: Money moves through me.
Out: Abundance is always available.

In: Everyone Wins!
Out: We are all in this together.

In: We are an aligned team.
Out: Love.

In: I keep my body healthy and happy.
Out: I am a model of responsibly caring for myself.

In: My income keeps increasing.
Out: There is more for *all* of us!

In: My life is aligned with service to Humanity.
Out: We can do it!

Overall, I feel a deep sense of Peace, Connectedness, and Service to Humanity with this holistic view of my intentions.

So now I have another question for you. In my qigong class, when we are starting a new move, my teacher often says to set the intention once and then let it go and relax into the movement. He says we don't need to keep setting the intention, or thinking of the intention, every time we repeat the move.

He also emphasizes acting with *confidence* that we are moving the energy the way we intend to.

I feel like I'm not always confident that I'm moving my milestone and flowing river intentions forward. I sometimes forget the words and the feel of them – especially the words and feel of this new aspect of the receiving and giving components of my intentions. Maybe this is why I've heard a lot of people using the practice of keeping their intentions written down in front of them, and reviewing them, speaking them, or somehow connecting with them at least once a day.

I guess my question is if I'll get to a point where I can set the intention and let it go?

II: This is a question of scale. Some intentions feel easy to you and are manifested fairly quickly in time-space. These are intentions that you can easily set, and let go, with confidence that they will manifest.

Imagine you are floating in the great big Intention Sea and you would like to manifest an intention that is the equivalent of pushing a wave of water from where you are to, say, five feet away from you.

You give the water a gentle push with your hand and let it go, fully confident it will reach the destination five feet away.

Let's say you are quite practiced at creating these intention waves that travel five-foot distances, and now you want to create an intention that will need to cross 100 feet of distance in order to manifest at the shore.

Me: How do I know how far an intention will need to travel in order to manifest?

II: Usually you have a sense of this because it feels like a "big deal" or it involves more moving parts, people, resources, or skills than you have at your immediate disposal.

Me: OK.

II: So, you are intending something bigger that has more "distance" to travel. The "muscles" you have built up in manifesting the smaller five-foot wave intentions will help you to create with confidence, but you might not be able to manifest your intention with one push of the water.

This is where a second push, or multiple, periodic pushes, are necessary in order to bring the intention into the world.

Me: How can I know if, or when, I need to give another push? And is "another push" equivalent to re-connecting with, repeating aloud, or re-reading my original intention?

II: Realistically, you are often giving many intention waves pushes in your Intention Sea. Just look at your list of milestone and flowing river intentions. See? Lots of ideas you are bringing to the world.

So, how do you know if one of your many intentions needs another push in order to manifest?

The best answer is for you to become more and more familiar with your attention, and how it feels when your attention "antennae" are outstretched, connected, and freely flowing with the Universe vs. how it feels when your attention "antennae" are contracted, pulled in, frenzied, or focused too fixedly on a perceived problem.

You might make a habit of reviewing your intentions periodically to see how you feel about each intention – just like in qigong how you continue to practice the movement of the energy. As the *core* element of this intention-review practice, increase your awareness of the sensations when your attention is free-flowing toward all your intentions. Also notice when your attention is not free-flowing – when it's stuck or confined by some resistance somewhere.

And yes, a "push" could be reconnecting, re-reading, or repeating out loud your intention. But, the method of "push" is not critical. In any form, a push of your intention wave increases the energy (and Power and Attention) toward that intention.

You might note here, that the push doesn't always originate with you. Sometimes you will become aware of the Universe flowing more in the direction of one of your intentions. Like maybe a new path of opportunity for action opens up that you had not seen before.

When your attention antennae are outstretched and free-flowing, it's easy for you to pick up on these intention pushes from the Universe. Then you can direct more of your attention toward that intention for the moment, since there is already additional support and momentum behind it.

Me: This all feels very in the flow. How do I ensure that I keep all my intentions moving forward when my attention is just on the one or two that have a forward momentum at the current moment?

Should I create a practice of regularly reviewing all my intentions to make sure I don't lose sight of them? I mean, without the structure of my weekly qigong class, and the commitments I have made to practicing regularly at home, I don't think I would have grown my "sea of chi" dan tien as much as I have. I would not have benefitted from the practice without, well, practicing.

I could say the same for my Avatar tools: without regular use and practice I would not have grown my Awareness and moved forward in Consciousness as much as I have with these tools.

II: Yes, a commitment to regular practice could be helpful for you. But, in the spirit of "No Rules" and "Lighten Up!", I encourage you to always create an intention practice that feels enjoyable to you. If it ever feels like a chore, or something you *have* to do, that's a good time to re-think your approach to your intention practice.

Me: So, it's kind of like what Joseph Campbell said in his *Power of Myth* interviews: "the whole point is to enjoy the *Rapture* of life!"?

II: Exactly!

DAY 74

Me: Looking at my Milestone and Flowing River Intentions again, and just taking a moment to breathe in my heart-space with them, I notice I feel more relaxed.

I think that seeing the giving-and-receiving aspects of my intentions, and the feel from our last conversation about letting my attention antennae flow freely across all my intentions, has helped me to be more confident and at ease that I'm on track with the manifestation of all my intentions.

There are still a few of them that my attention lingers on – like a feeling that there might be an obstacle or stuckness in that area that I could explore in order to support an even easier flow of energy in that direction. But overall, I really have a sense that everything is all right and I'm right on track.

In fact, the feeling reminds me of one of my favorite Hafiz quotes:

> This place where you are right now,
> God circled on a map for you.

From this perspective of Peaceful "on-track-ness," what is next for us? How do I help bring you to the world? And how does your exposure in the world create more Clarity, Curiosity, and Harmony?

II: Yes, I too feel as though we are about ready for a change in approach for bringing "The Intention Idea" into the World. We have covered a lot of ground in our explorations together, and there will *always* be more for us to explore and share perspectives about as you humans continue to evolve and grow your awareness and skills at intention-creation. Our conversation and our relationship never ends, even if this is the last moment that you put pen to paper for this experience. We are connected.

How you bring me to the world will continue to morph and change, based on what is needed in the present moment. Stay open to the *many* possibilities, and take action on whatever next step calls to you in the moment.

As for the Clarity, Curiosity, and Harmony that is gifted to the world as a result of receiving me, well, each person who works with me will have their own experiences of these aspects, and their own stories to tell.

What have you noticed?

Me: I definitely feel more clarity about how to work with intentions. It's a really peaceful clarity too – not like a mental, logical, to-do list, but more like a deep inner knowing that, no matter what happens, I have the tools and resources to be able to successfully navigate my intention-creating. I felt that same feeling after taking the Avatar courses – like no matter what happens, I have the skills and resources to manage my responses and make the best of it.

I guess with this intention exploration, I feel another aspect of confidence in my actions and thoughts.

And I've *definitely* enjoyed our explorations and your perspectives on how to work with intentions. Based on how kindly you have always responded to me – even when I am deep in the "busy mind" – I feel I can easily continue to be curious and ask you anything. Yes, I definitely feel well-supported for ongoing explorations together.

As for harmony, when you first talked about harmony at the beginning of our conversations together, I had a mental picture of being and acting in harmony with other people.

But now, when I think of harmony, it feels more like connectedness with the Whole Universe – all the energies, ideas, intentions, and flows of attention that intermingle in this sea of experience. I feel like harmony with all-that-is is not a utopian concept for me anymore, but a deliberate way of being that results from a continued

THE INTENTION IDEA

practice of intention-work.

I feel ready to show up and play my unique instruments and melodies in concert with the greater, entire orchestra of life.

Wow! Just saying that feels like a big commitment! But it also feels like a recognition of what we *all* are always doing – I'm just taking even more responsibility for the role and part I'm playing now.

II: Rock on!

Me: I so enjoy your sense of humor and lightness!

II: My energy and perspectives are always available to you – to *all* of you. Reach out, connect, ask a question, share a perspective, and *enjoy* creating your intentions.

The enjoyment is where it's at!

♡

RESOURCES

There are so many giants on whose shoulders I stand. Rather than overwhelm you with a long list, here are a few of my top favorites that I mention throughout the book:

The Avatar Courses, by Harry Palmer and delivered through Star's Edge International®. Learn more at https://avatarepc.com

Books by Harry Palmer (easily found at http://avatarbookstore.com)

The Avatar Path: The Way We Came

Living Deliberately: The Discovery and Development of Avatar

Private Lessons

The Avatar Legacy

ReSurfacing: Techniques for Exploring Consciousness

Big Magic, by Elizabeth Gilbert. Such great perspectives about creating with ideas.

A Light Warrior's Guide to High Level Energy Healing, by Michael Lomax. This gem is written by my qigong teacher's teacher and current lineage holder of the Stillness-Movement Neigong system.

Qigong with my teacher, Ben Rosen in Portland, Oregon: https://www.qilinherbs.com

The Field, by Lynne McTaggart. Interesting experiments that demonstrate the quantum field and our connectedness beyond the visible reality.

The Millionaire Course, by Marc Allen. Lots of inspiring approaches and affirmations around money and creating your ideal life.

The Type-Z Guide To Success, by Marc Allen. Another favorite from Marc that incorporates practical manifestation techniques while staying aligned with the Flow of Life.

The Dynamic Laws of Prosperity, by Catherine Ponder. Original ideas for visualization and affirmation techniques.

The Gabriel Method, by Jon Gabriel. The source of the abundance visualization I used for money. Great meditations and ideas for creating your ideal body.

ACKNOWLEDGMENTS

This book would not have come into existence without the support and life-altering impact of many people on my life. To list a few feels like I leave out so many, so if you don't see your name here, but you know me, thank you for all the ways you have touched my life.

To Dan Coppersmith, love of my life, thank you for appreciating me no matter what, for always having my back, for your thoughtful edits, and well, for everything.

To Harry Palmer and the entire Star's Edge crew, thank you for the amazing tools for navigating my life so clearly, for all the appreciation while untangling from stuck creations, for all the opportunities to fully realize my life purpose, and for your never-ending efforts to co-create an Enlightened Planetary Civilization®.

To Christina Frei, thank you for your unbridled enthusiasm, your camaraderie, and your recognition of how sacred this work is, for all of us.

To Mom, thank you for introducing me to the fine art of automatic writing and making sure I'm tuning in to energies that serve me well.

To Cathi Hutchison, my book cover artist, thank you for translating a feeling into an image so that anyone can get a sense of *The Intention Idea* right from the start.

ABOUT THE AUTHOR

Melissa Cantrelle is a beloved author of inspired works. Her Big Heart and keen ability to discern, sort, and organize thoughts and emotions have led her to be a writer of books that are both uplifting and practical. She is fascinated by things that help her and humanity evolve and move forward. This passion led her to become a licensed Avatar master: helping others attain the Avatar tools for managing the mind and awakening the Spirit, and dedicated to co-creating an Enlightened Planetary Civilization®. Melissa currently lives near Portland, Oregon with her mate Dan. You can reach her via http://melissacantrelle.com.

From Melissa:
"I hope that my ways of expressing perspectives serve to lift you up and inspire you to whatever next steps are best for you. If something I've said doesn't work for you right now, I encourage you to just take what resonates for you and let the rest be where it is on the page. May you be Happy & Well!"

www.ingramcontent.com/pod-product-compliance
Lightning Source LLC
LaVergne TN
LVHW051550070426
835507LV00021B/2497